Innopreneur

101 Chronicles on How Circumstance, Preparation
and Brilliance Advance Innovation

edited by
Ton Langeler

Published in the United States by Channel V Books,
a division of Channel V Media, New York, NY.
www.ChannelVBooks.com

Channel V Books and its logo are trademarks of Channel V Media.
ISBN 978-0-9824739-9-3

Library of Congress Control Number: 2011943223

Library of Congress subject headings:
Organizational Innovation.
Innovation.
Entrpreneurship.

PRINTED IN THE UNITED STATES OF AMERICA

10 9 8 7 6 5 4 3 2 1

First Edition

for Arthur Antonius Maclure

"Este libro no es más que eso, sólo un libro.
Personal y subjetivo, como la relación que une a un padre con su hijo;
pero por eso mismo universal como la relación entre padre e hijo,
la más común de todas."

FERNANDO SAVATER, "ética para amador"

All profits from this book will be donated to charity to support microcredits,
which put entrepreneurship within reach for those with little or no access to capital.

Contents

Introduction

Putting a plan into action is often tougher than the theory suggests. A defensive approach is often applied that seeks to minimize possible mistakes. Yet for innovation, it is essential to increase the chances and opportunities to create added value for the user and the initiator.

Invention and innovation are closely related—two sides of the same coin, really—but there's a distinct difference between the two. Whereas an invention emerges as a one-off solution to a problem, innovation builds upon this solution and makes it available to the user. An invention is limited in reach if not paired with strategic deployment that will bring it into mainstream awareness. Innovation, on the other hand, is precisely that: the translation of an idea into a product or service, which is then brought to market in a way that allows it to spread far and wide.

The invention-innovation conversation can be likened to the one about the old tree in the forest: if it falls and no one is around to hear it, does it really make a sound? The world may never know...and that's precisely the problem. Now, if invention is the tree that falls in the empty forest, then innovation must be the *same* tree in the *same* forest, only it's fallen in the presence of a number of stunned onlookers. These witnesses eliminate the question of sound, while their absence leaves sound up to eternal debate.

Just like the lone tree, a lone invention can introduce high costs and no benefit. Innovation guarantees that invention is "heard," and is therefore its sustainable equivalent.

This book explores invention and innovation from the perspective of their respective relationships with the commercial marketplace. It then goes a step further, applying this line of thought to the almost parallel world of entrepreneurship.

Entrepreneurs, like a good idea or invention, are only as successful as their delivery strategy. This fact explains why some startups stall while others thrive, and why the same idea is shelved by one and brought into fruition by another—independent of the merit (or lack thereof) of the original concept.

The truth is that there are no original ideas. A great idea—whether applied to a product or business initiative—is the chance meeting of circumstances, preparation and brilliance. And while this seemingly serendipitous meeting occurs under very specific conditions, it is rare that a single person experiences it in isolation. Knowing this to be the case, one wonders what it is that separates those who are successful bringing it to market and those who are unable to give concrete and commercially-viable form to their otherwise abstract ideas. In the case of the innovative entrepreneur—or *Innopreneur*—the same person who is responsible for the idea is also very often responsible for its delivery to market.

101 experts from across the globe have joined forces to give concrete form to this international project. Their not-so-humble challenge was to explore the commonalities between entrepreneurship and innovation, all through the lens of Innovation. And from there, to define the patterns, traits, and nuances that contribute to success in its delivery.

By distilling innovation down to its empirical elements, these experts offer managers and entrepreneurs insight they can apply to their businesses in pursuit of replicable and scalable success.

The articles in this book appear in alphabetic order of author's surname. For reading about specific subjects, an index of Articles by Topic is provided at the end of this book.

Note from the Editor

Over the years, several people have asked me for a checklist of things to do when launching new product ideas into the market. I've provided numerous sets of questions to help people plan their efforts to bring ideas alive, and I have myself been eager to learn how to become more successful in delivering innovations to customers and consumers. Recently, however, I have taken a different approach. Rather than collecting know-how in the form of business cases and of both new theories and practical experiences from clients, colleagues, papers, magazines and notes during conferences and presentations, I have asked the experts to write their learnings in short and inspirational articles. The result of this journey is this book, which I would like to share with you.

A few things led me to the goal of collecting the views of some great minds and experienced practitioners on how to deliver innovation. One of them was a presentation I attended not so long ago by Stephen King of Swiss-based multinational Nestlé. His main message was that innovation project management is the new area for corporate development, as only with this focus can companies increase their hit rate of new product introductions. He reiterated my sentiment that it is not the lack of good product ideas, but the lack of preparation for the execution of these ideas that is leading to a successful innovation.

Guus Berkhout, an acknowledged professor from the Technical University Delft, once shared with me his idea that it is not enough to *take* risks when you want to innovate, you have to *search* for them. This is because only in uncertainty lies the bliss of discovery.

A few years ago, I met Paul France, an enthusiastic Procter & Gamble director. He introduced himself as an "innovation entrepreneur" though he was an employee on the payroll of the multinational. But, indeed, why can't employees be entrepreneurs? In fact, I wish that every company had a few entrepreneurial minds focused on reaching for a better world and making the impossible possible (and providing the business with sustainable growth).

This "innovation entrepreneur" explained the protection program that P&G purposefully installed to stimulate calculated risk-taking—they must have had the same teacher as "genius Guus." People who dare to take calculated risks need to not only be able to find some form or other of compensation, but also operate from some sort of stable basis. You can accept uncertainties if, in other areas, you can remain planted on firm ground. What these entrepreneurs need is not a license to take any old risk, but some sort of guard against innovation terrorists (i.e., conservatives who not only kill new ideas but also try to damage those brave pioneers who are eager to realize the seemingly impossible). On micro and macro economic levels this could translate into, among other things, clear regulations, which, in reality, are rare.

On the other side, innovators just have to go for it and persevere. You can't make everybody happy if you want to innovate. As Thijs Kramer, a Dutch politician, said; "Seeking consensus is the enemy of ambition." This, of course, is not to say that you shouldn't share your ideas. Quite the contrary, in fact...

In her brilliant article in the book *The Age of Conversation*, Jessica Hagy poetically and passionately echoes this sentiment: "Spit it out! That is how you make it real...If you have a marvelous idea, put it in the spotlight... Tell her you love her before someone else does...Ideas kept secret don't succeed...Let it out where it can grow and spread and thrive."

In many perspectives, two general phases are often identified in innovation processes; the Fuzzy Front End and the Stage-Gate® Process, of which the last one is seen as disciplinary expertise in project management. Research by Abbie Griffin of the University of Utah shows that these perspectives are insufficient to describe how successful breakthrough innovations are delivered. A team should not consider their work complete after having simply defined an innovative concept. They should also seek to execute it. They not only shepherd the concept through additional development to a commercialized product, but also typically work to drive market acceptance as well. And one should be able to circle back to earlier stages and operate more flexibly (in a less disciplined way) than more traditional views of the innovation process suggest.

In my work, I have shared many of my personal, experience-based convictions of how to improve innovation efforts and shared my varying success. I don't want to claim that my counsel always leads to happier managers, but I strongly believe that solid research in combination with real life examples lead to better decisions. I bring readers this combination—not via my own stories, but directly from the 101+ experts who have contributed *their* stories and real-life examples.

If anything in this book leads to new learning or experience—which is my sincere goal—I hope you will share the resulting insights and stories.

Finally, I have to say that I am delighted to be able to donate all the profits of this book to charity to promote entrepreneurship among those in poverty. I am convinced that such support (and pay back; it is just a small loan) is much more sustainable than "gifts." My thanks go to all contributors, who so very kindly provided their views without any obligations!

Definitions and Restrictions

The delivery of innovation is a business *supernova*. It's the ultimate form of cumulative energy; an explosion of collaboration, a unifier of disparate activities and a creator of synergy among multiple areas of expertise. It's also a challenge—one that requires its practitioners to convince others that change, innovation's defining characteristic, is not only good, but necessary. Delivering innovation to the marketplace entails first breaking through conservative barriers and transcending storms within the organization where the ideas are born.

Because inventing new solutions exhausts resources and costs money, the goal of doing so should be based on achieving economic transactions. Innovation is the process and act through which inventions are introduced to the market with this goal in mind. Innovation, in other words, is the sustainable equivalent of invention.

For the purpose of this project, Innovation Delivery (ID) is defined as that which is necessary for turning an idea or invention into a commercial success.

In this context, ID is the back-end of innovation and is linked to the fuzzy front-end. Although my direct colleagues and I are not convinced of the necessity of a fixed, sequential innovation process (and therefore restricting creativity to its first stage), it could be said that ID comes after innovation strategy, ideation and/or spontaneous discoveries. ID comprises concept development and technological development (or product development). It does *not* include fundamental research, strategic planning, blue ocean ideation or the definition of battlefields and/or innovation platforms. "Delivery" is therefore broader than market implementation; it encompasses the entire execution, including conceptual fine-tuning, prototyping, upscaling, market introduction and after-care.

Innovation, in this context, is perhaps somewhat contentiously defined as, "The process of converting something new—an idea or invention—into a sustainable market success."

Acknowledgements

Our sincere thanks go to all of the enthusiastic and willing contributors who offered their insight and expertise to this initiative. Without them, this book simply would not exist. Their involvement not only exemplifies their entrepreneurial spirits (they dove in not knowing where this project would lead: it also showcases their integrity and leadership. By staying loyal to their distinct perspectives—which are reflected in the often-passionate and always-thoughtful articles that comprise this book—they have offered this topic the richness and depth it deserves.

We would also like to thank a few people who have been of particular help throughout, beginning with Leonne van den Heuvel. Leonne has supported this project with her hard work, mental support and unshakeable confidence in our approach...which carried us along when responses were scarce and spirits were low.

We owe our gratitude to Tori Kelly for her extensive language editing and the vast supply of spot-on expressions she lent us along the way.

We greatly appreciate the design and web support provided to us by Lex Staver.

We thank Gretel Going and the team at Channel V Books for their key role in bringing this book to market with innovative technology and wide distribution channels.

Many others have been instrumental in the realization of this initiative, either by offering extra support during its initiation or their encouragement and creative suggestions along the way. Four people we'd like to mention by name are Patrick van der Duin (Delft University of Technology), Fusien Verloop (Leenaers Verloop), Heske Verburg (UNICEF) and Christina Hepner Brodie (PDMA).

A number of contributors and friends have offered us valuable advice, or have introduced us to additional hard-to reach contributors. In particular, we thank Kitty Leering, Erna Möller, Jorrit van der Togt, Pierre van Hedel, Muriel Wateler and Paul Hobcraft. And of course Joanna. You have all been of great support.

I would like to thank everyone I've worked with over the last decade. In one way or another, they have inspired me—whether with their (often direct) opinions and honest views on innovation delivery and change management, or their general interest in and passion for the subject.

Thank you.

Answering Three Questions That Determine Innovation Success

Scott D. Anthony

Many companies struggling with innovation point the finger at a lack of good ideas, but that's rarely the real problem. Most are overflowing with good ideas; the difficulty is their inability to translate good ideas into good businesses.

The core problem stems from their insistence in turning innovation into an academic exercise: they study...and plan...and debate...and plan...and pontificate...and study...and plan. The output of this exercise is a detailed business plan, with dense logic and comprehensive financials, not innovation. All too often these types of plans fail to survive upon contact with the marketplace. The financial model that worked so well on paper turns out to have a fatal flaw. The market research that showed high degrees of customer willingness to pay doesn't pan out. The timeline that engineering signed off on turns out to be a flight of fancy.

Thomas Edison was right when he said, "Genius is one percent inspiration, 99 percent perspiration." The challenging aspect of innovation isn't the thinking; it's the doing.

Companies should honestly assess their answers to the following three questions, which ultimately determine business success:

Does anyone want it?
If your answer to this question is based on market surveys, you actually know very little. If your answer is based on giving people an early prototype and asking them if they would buy it, you actually know very little. You don't know much about demand until someone spends money to purchase something or invests time to use something.

Can you deliver it?
If your answer to this question is based on feasibility studies, you actually know very little. Find ways to develop proof of concept prototypes as quickly as possible. Run a small-scale pilot to see what happens when your entire

operational system comes together. You are quite likely to encounter something you didn't anticipate. Seek to unearth these unknown variables as soon as possible.

Do the numbers work?
If your answer to this question is based on an Excel model, you actually know very little. Find a way to earn your first dollar (or rupee or RMB or Euro) of revenue. Zero in on your idea's unit economics. Actual results will give you a clearer picture of your idea's potential.

It's never been easier to do this. For example, in 2008 we had an idea for a new laundry services business in India. Thirty days later, our first customer paid us 68 rupees (about 1.25 dollars) to wash their clothes and deliver them the next day. Experts on eLance.com can help you create a visualization of your idea in a week. Lower 3D printing costs allow rough prototypes of physical products to be made more quickly. Turn innovation from an academic to a hands-on activity, and you'll increase the odds of turning great ideas into great businesses.

Scott D. Anthony leads Innosight's venture capital investing activities and Asian operations. He is the author of The Little Black Book of Innovation. *blogs.hbr.org/anthony/*

Entrepreneurial Spirit Is Needed

Jan Peter Balkenende

Claudia Willemsen, a young mother, was surfing the Internet for quality children's clothes, and realized she didn't like anything she saw online. So what did she do? Claudia refused to accept the situation and began trading clothes on the Web in 2003, dubbing her business Kleertjes.com. Her online shop instantly "hit the charts". She now employs a staff of 125, serving approximately 100,000 customers, and she was recently presented with the Porsche Female Entrepreneur of the Year Award for her business drive and initiative—a well-deserved token of appreciation for her efforts and perseverance. No less than 50 women, who had all set up businesses of their own, have been nominated for the Award.

What does Claudia's story—and that of all other startup entrepreneurs, male or female—teach us? I believe it's all about three basic elements: creativity, entrepreneurial spirit and networking.

Creativity is about having ideas, an instinct for understanding market niches and making plans. It's also a vital factor in wanting to make your dreams come true. Entrepreneurial spirit helps get things off the ground in order to outperform the competition and cope with setbacks, so you and your business can achieve maximum potential. Networking is essential because it's impossible to achieve things totally on your own. Entrepreneurs need to network with buyers, knowledge centers, suppliers, large businesses, and financiers. Networks are decisive in turning good ideas, allied with an entrepreneurial attitude, into success stories.

Obviously, innovation can be stimulated: by talking about it in schools, giving appealing examples and facilitating it in various other ways. I remember when the Innovation Platform in the Netherlands was trying to figure out how small and medium-sized enterprises could benefit more from available sources of knowledge around them. This resulted in our decision to introduce "Innovation Vouchers", which those enterprises could use to purchase information from universities or colleges. And they include not only tax facilities or accelerated procedures (for permits, for instance), but also putting informed workers from other countries to work much faster. All of it is necessary, but at the end of the day it comes down to three elements: creativity, entrepreneurial spirit and networking.

Once a business has been set up, activity growth and expansion are key. The Netherlands has a great many startups that somehow fail to grow, which reminds me of what top-class athletes often say: "Getting to the top is one thing, but staying there is a lot more difficult." This also holds true for startups. Sound entrepreneurship demands that you stay abreast of market trends and know what your business has to offer in that light. Sustainability should be a top priority—there's no two ways about it. Companies that can bring together innovation, sustainability and entrepreneurship in an original way, making corporate social responsibility an obvious choice, will dominate tomorrow's corporate scene. It's no coincidence that General Motors, which was in dire straits a few years back, has chosen an electric car as an instrument to safeguard its future. Last but not least, there's the international angle: power and economic welfare are being redistributed. Asia, the BRICs economies, emerging markets—everything is changing in top gear. Entrepreneurship means capitalizing on those new trends.

Startups are facing huge challenges and opportunities at the beginning of the twenty-first century. Though it may not be easy, the right blend of creativity, entrepreneurial spirit and networking will go a long way. So go out and make the most of it!

Jan Peter Balkenende is the former Prime Minister of the Kingdom of the Netherlands, Partner at Ernst & Young and Professor of Governance, Institutions and Internationalization at the Erasmus University Rotterdam. www.ey.nl

Innovation from Frustration

Niels Bark

With a talented young development team and a fresh business approach, Vanmoof has only one goal: to help the ambitious global urbanite bike around the city with style.

In the Netherlands we've been riding bikes for centuries—even our royal family rides them! Yet the Dutch market hasn't had much to offer in terms of an urban-proof bike: a bike able to withstand weather, daily use, and the occasional touch of vandalism. Of course, it's not particularly easy for a bike to be completely urban-proof, but the entrepreneurial brothers Taco and Ties Carlier couldn't understand why urban needs seemed to be so ignored. Stores were flooded with complicated bikes that made a simple tool far too prone to failure.

Having developed successful products for Strida-Europe and Dutchband BV, the brothers approached 100 friends from various cities and asked them what they considered the ultimate commuter tool. The response—a sexy, durable and affordable bike—became Vanmoof's challenge. The friends tested 100 prototypes for 100 days, and the foundations for Vanmoof were laid. The company decided to turn the backbone of Dutch culture inside out, stripping the bike of any non-essentials that could break or cause frustration, and adding features within the big, lightweight aluminum tubing. The signature Vanmoof look was born.

Vanmoof strives for optimal efficiency within its product design process, and four industrial designers work closely with the entire Vanmoof team. This collaboration has enabled the company to bring three brand new models, including three major innovations and a patent design, to the market within two years.

Vanmoof's design process was a result of being frustrated by both the traditional approach of the bicycle industry and the lack of interaction with end-users. For instance, standard locks frustrated bicyclists due to the problem of lock storage while riding. After questioning its target audience through social media (amongst other means), Vanmoof joined forces with ABUS and came up with a solution: integrating the lock into the frame. Collaboration with specialized partners ensures a fast, efficient product innovation process—and has given Vanmoof the opportunity to concentrate on developing the ultimate city bike.

Niels Bark, *Vanmoof Bicycles*

A Perfect Life:
Ten Unconventional Golden Rules

Jon Barrett

Innovation is like a disability: innovators see problems everywhere, which drives them by an inner force to find solutions. Like gambling, innovation is addictive; with occasional highs outweighing the predicable lows. To make innovation fun and profitable, it needs to be controlled. What is innovation? Simple—it's the commercial viability of something that's never been done before.

Here are some of my unconventional golden rules—they may be the opposite of what you've been taught, but they work for me.

Go to market right now, TODAY.
You can always find reasons to not launch your innovation. Ignore them all— pretend your prototype is the final product and go to market **now**! Being first to market is a huge barrier to future competition. If your product is truly innovative, your customers have nothing to compare it to and won't even realize it's a prototype. If it offers them benefits they'll thank you for getting it to them ASAP, and you get early revenue.

Ignore focus groups, even yourself...listen to your customers.
Book a cheap stand at an exhibition, place your prototype on show and let the public play with it. Watch what they do, listen to what they say, and build your sales pitch around what you learn.

Then stop listening, stop tinkering and start selling.
There comes a point when you've heard enough feedback and done enough design tweaking—it can't go on forever! When this happens, take a break from innovating and immerse yourself in sales. Take the money and enjoy it.

Price high and see what happens.
Innovations are hard to price because if they're truly new, it's impossible to run meaningful comparisons. With our product we initially launched at £1 per credit: no one bought. At 50p still no one bought. At 35p we sold to early adopters. Once we dropped to 25p, the floodgates suddenly opened. Our

customers decided 25p per credit was what our product was worth—pricing made easy!

Trash your intellectual property.
Intellectual property is useful if either you plan to sell your business or you have the money to defend it. Selling wasn't part of my business plan; I didn't have the money to defend my intellectual property, and as software innovation I couldn't patent it even if I wanted to. So I went to market, saving both time and money. Getting to market first is the greatest defense of innovators, creators, and pathfinders. We do what no one else can, we break the rules...everyone else is just a lazy imitator. Customers love being part of the story—they love backing the winner.

Beg for competitors—the more the better.
Customers are scared of innovations, frightened of the unknown. Get to market first, and then pray for competitors. Copycat products validate your idea by making the purchasing decision easier and safer. Customers like to know they have choice, and armed with that knowledge they will choose the leader.

Support the strong and destroy the weak.
Some innovations want to live; others want to die. A poorly conceived, badly assembled prototype will work like a charm, and keep on working no matter how badly you treat it—that innovation deserves to live. A well-designed and perfectly manufactured prototype will fail and fail again despite constant attention and repair. That innovation wants to die; kill it now before it wastes your time. Learn how to spot the innovations worth supporting.

Beware of phantom problems.
Innovators see problems everywhere: they can't help it. Differentiate between problems that people will spend money on overcoming, and problems that people will tolerate. The former brings great wealth, the latter disappointment and failure.

Rest—then innovate again.
Solving one problem often creates another. After monetizing your first innovation, take time to rest your mind. Then identify where the problem has 'moved' to and get back to work, this time using your past experience to function more quickly and efficiently.

Find out where you think best and spend quality time there.
There's usually one place and time where you think most clearly: the bath, car, bed, hotel, holiday, etc. Isolate this space and make time to be there. Then read, think and innovate: a perfect life.

Jon Barrett, Publishing Research Laboratories, Kent, UK, purelabs.co.uk

Hashtag Innovation

Gerbrand Bas

Even on Twitter, innovation is a sustainable trending topic. A constant flow of tweets with the innovation hashtag flashes by as you scroll down. Innovation is truly alive and kicking. But a closer look reveals a great deal of worry in those 140 characters; innovation is hard, and Innovating is even harder. Writing and philosophizing about it is one thing, but doing it is quite another thing entirely.

Of course, there's always incremental innovation. A good look at the Dutch annual NRC Top 100 most innovative SMEs can lead to the conclusion that there's a lot of decent innovation going on in the Netherlands. But if you're looking for real breakthrough innovations, you'll be hard pushed. Hardcore innovation needs to be sought after with a microscope because even within the first ten companies mentioned in this yearly review, I counted exactly zero. Seven companies have amazingly clever process innovations, there's one impressive system innovation and two cool product innovations...but if your standards are higher and you want fundamental innovations, you are out of luck. The NRC Top 100 proves that the needs of true innovation connoisseurs are rarely fulfilled in the Netherlands.

Time is needed for the real work to get done—time, money, patience, and coincidence. The latter is especially hard to steer. Time is scarce, and money is becoming harder to find every day. This all leads to uncertainty because innovating is crucial; without innovation there is no future. This has been researched and calculated over and over again. We're aware of the knowledge paradox; we know that innovating cannot be learned, and that venture capital rather than risk capital and subsidies all too often don't work. We need companies like TomTom—not just one, but lots of them. Any new policy falls back to this mantra over and over again. Just look at Finland: they're doing well! Or rather they did it well, like the Dutch used to when we stuck Fokker airplanes together. You see, the Dutch know how to innovate.

At least, the Dutch can innovate if (as my mother used say) they want to. Don't we want it then? Of course we do, but we're going about it the hard way and seem a bit lost. We're not doing what we're good at, we don't know the full extent of our knowledge and we answer the wrong questions. We're acting like banks, who (along with their clients) seemed to have lost track of what they're here for. Savings products, each more innovative than the next, are all well and good but in the end impossible for anyone to understand.

In the same way, we Dutch let ourselves be held hostage by a combination of regulations and sky-high ambitions until someone proves that things are just a little bit different in practice, and simple is already complicated enough. Take serial entrepreneur Ruud Koornstra, for example. At a frantic speed, he starts one company after another, always inspired and animated and not afraid to make mistakes—and ever so often he does make mistakes. This preacher of sustainable innovation, who seeks surprise and amazement, spots opportunities everywhere.

Follow twitter hashtag innovation—the next breakthrough is already being prepared.

Gerbrand Bas is director of Designlink. @GerbrandBas

End-To-End Creativity
in the Innovation Process

Jeffrey Baumgartner

In the organizational innovation process, creativity is typically exerted only at the beginning. You generate a lot of ideas, identify the best ones and implement them. But think about it. When was the last time you launched a project in which things didn't go wrong at almost *every* step of the way?

Learning Curve
Every new project involves a learning curve as unanticipated problems arise. The bigger and more complex the project, the bigger and more complex the resulting problems are. Innovative projects, by their nature, involve new techniques and approaches that inevitably result in unexpected challenges during implementation.

Imagine that the founders of a company dream up a creative new product idea. Brainstorming sessions and focus group discussions develop it into an innovative concept. The design is completed and presented to the production team, but a key component can't be made with existing tools. Ideally, the production people would bring together a diverse team and brainstorm alternatives that add value. In practice, either they look for a quick fix, outsource or decide to invest in new equipment—any of which delays the project immensely.

Meanwhile, the legal department discovers that legislation in a key market would prevent the product from being sold as is. Here's another opportunity to frame the problem as a creative challenge and brainstorm for solutions, but this seldom happens. The lawyers and project manager seek a more conventional solution, perhaps dropping the project altogether.

If you reflect on innovative projects you've worked on, you can probably think of similar instances. Projects get a creative start, but little creative continuity. Why is this? There are three reasons.

- We tend to see the innovation process as a creative one primarily during the conception stage of a project.

- Managers are seldom taught or encouraged to approach operational or project development problems in a creative way. Moreover, many managers fear that communicating a need for creative problem solving would indicate a failure or lack of competence on their part.

- Many innovation tools are designed to capture ideas from the entire workforce, yet lack the functionality to enable specific teams to focus on specific problems.

Opportunities Knock

Projects don't just cause problems—sometimes they provide opportunities. For instance, a software programmer might observe that a new software product could be easily integrated with popular email software, providing more functionality without additional cost. A manufacturing person might notice that a product being made for a specific purpose could also be used for a completely different objective, potentially doubling the market.

A business partner who manufactures parts to order may identify ways to make their parts less expensive, lighter or available in a wider range of colors. However, unless they're involved in your innovation process, they'll just keep on building to order rather than suggest alternatives.

Lost Opportunities

What this all means is that while many projects start off as the result of intense creative thinking, that creativity is not applied throughout the lifetime of the implementation process. Typically, Managers and others involved in the process are neither encouraged nor given the tools to apply creative thinking to problem solving. Likewise, there are seldom tools or a procedure for those involved in implementation to try alternative ideas once the process begins.

Fortunately, there's an easy solution: don't just use creativity before you launch a project, but throughout the entire project. Progress meetings can be used to discuss problems, opportunities and creative solutions. Managers who identify problems and teams that solve them should be rewarded. In short, apply creativity at all phases of the project lifetime.

Jeffrey Baumgartner is the author of The Way of the Innovation Master, *inventor of Jenni innovation process management software and founder of jpb.com companies. http://www.jpb.com.*

Good Project Teams Are Key to Innovation Success

Titus Bekkering

Projects have been the preferred mode for achieving innovations over the past few decades, to the extent that pre-defined Stage-Gate® Processes are found all over the corporate innovation landscape. These so-called funnels provide a road map for the various disciplines involved on coordinating their activities, and they all aim for the Holy Grail: getting a new product or service successfully launched on the market. They're rationally designed and perfectly sensible—a recipe for success. Yet the success rate of innovations leaves a lot to be desired. What's the disconnect?

In 2008 Dutch-based p2project management, The Rotterdam School of Management at Erasmus University and innovation agency pro-Actuate teamed up in the Netherlands to investigate this disconnect among some 60 businesses in different sectors. The study focused on the process of idea selection, development, testing, upscaling and launch. The results showed that the vast majority of the respondents (80%) would like to double their innovation success, and strive for a renewal rate increase (percentage of business derived from recent innovations) of approximately 30%. Those who are content with their innovation rate have already achieved a 30% renewal rate. What sets the successful innovators apart?

The same pre-defined Stage-Gate® Processes were also common amongst less successful innovators, so that's not the answer. What set the successful innovators apart were a few common elements similar to a car ride: a driver, some passengers, fuel and a journey without too many long stops.

The Driver
Innovations often contain either some form of new technology, a market innovation, or both. It's common practice that a specialist with extensive knowledge of the most important innovation aspects is appointed to run the project. The study, however, indicated that businesses that focus their project manager selection on ambition and talent for leadership are significantly more successful in innovation than those who pick the best "content specialist." Leaders are able to drive projects forward and overcome hurdles.

The Passengers

But the driver's seat isn't the only important factor. In fact, all the seats and their occupants are crucial. Businesses that pay attention to team chemistry, as well as the knowledge on content required for the project, achieve a significantly higher innovation success rate. Complementary team roles are useful for overcoming hurdles; just like a car ride, the journey is much smoother if the kids aren't fighting in the back seat.

The Fuel

The third significant parameter was the personal "fuel" for the team. Businesses that provide opportunities for their teams to personally share in an innovation's success do markedly better.

The Journey

Does all that ensure a swift journey in our car? Not yet. Another factor that distinguishes the successful innovators from their competition is quicker decision making. Inefficient decisions often slow things down. Poor decision makers can at times force the car off the road, prescribe a detour, insist on a coffee break or even take the car to the garage for a painstaking examination. This not only makes for slower development, but also has an effect on the innovation's success in the market.

The study results underline that innovation requires complex team play that cannot be caught up in pre-defined processes. Funnels don't work—people do.

Titus Bekkering is managing partner of p2 project management, which specializes in innovation delivery projects and development of required organizational competencies. www.p2.nl

Venture Capital Supports Innovative Product Launch

Anthony Di Benedetto, Roger J. Calantone

New entrepreneurial ventures face many challenges in commercializing radical innovations. First, the entrepreneur deals with resource constraints. Unlike larger, more established firms with corporate new product development (NPD) funding and a large talent base, the entrepreneur only has limited startup funding and the skills of the founding team at his or her disposal. Second, the entrepreneur is an unknown entity and therefore a risky investment for venture capitalists and other investors, yet paradoxically dependent on these investors for support and even survival. This paradox has been called the *liability of newness* by researcher Arthur Stinchcombe. Clearly the entrepreneur must overcome the liability of newness and attract sufficient venture capital in order to increase the chances of survival and success.

In the rush to obtain startup capital to get their venture going, entrepreneurs must not ignore the importance of a successful launch. The costs and risks of a new product launch are daunting; yet our review of new product launch literature shows that little academic research has focused specifically on launch issues. Much of what we know derives from studying larger firms, who face different levels of uncertainty. In our study of venture capital funding for new entrepreneurial ventures, we find that applying venture capital at the time of the innovation's launch is of prime importance.

Unlike larger firms, startup ventures have a single product and thus a single large risk to manage. This risk is managed by reducing the probability of loss: getting smarter, learning by doing and acquiring knowledge from suppliers and intended channel members. Learning from the downstream channel ensures launch success. This expansion of knowledge is achieved from loosely coupled networks consisting of those looking for new things to sell as well as venture capitalists and bankers who are betting on the venture's success and referring the seller to channels that have previously paid off. So the venture capitalists not only invest but also exert pressure to connect with optimal information links. As such, a well-funded launch must also be a knowledgeable launch.

We obtained a sample of 334 entrepreneurial startups involved in high and moderate tech innovation. We asked respondents to rate their resource and skill levels in both market research and sales force/distribution, as well as to assess their market orientation levels (to what extent they obtained and used customer and competitor information). We expected high marketing resources, skills and customer market orientation to increase launch capabilities (good communication and distribution effort, targeted to the right customers), which would increase the quality of distribution, channel coordination, and promotion for the launch. We hypothesized that high launch capability and quality would be associated with better innovation performance measured by market share, sales, returns, and breakeven time, and this was indeed the case. We also ran controls for innovation type and tested for interactions between launch capability and launch quality, but they were insignificant.

It's important to recognize that venture capital's presence not only funds capabilities, but also adds additional knowledge nets to reduce risk and ensure a smart launch. Venture capital presence impacted both launch capability and performance, significantly affecting the effect size of launch quality and capability.

The managerial lesson for entrepreneurs is to recognize the impact of venture capital on the success of their radical innovations. Inflow of venture capital increases the entrepreneur's ability to commercialize the product successfully. While there is much emphasis placed on obtaining venture capital and using it to start the new venture's operations, the quality boost that capital investment can provide the launch cannot be ignored by the entrepreneur.

Anthony Di Benedetto teaches at Temple University and Technische Universiteit Eindhoven.
Roger J. Calantone teaches at Michigan State University.

Successful Innovation from a Garden Shed

Glenn Bijvoets

Innovation realization has its own dynamics and function, and deserves a special place within an organization. This is especially seen in the positioning, connection and design of innovation. Whether your organization resembles a 1970s end-terrace house, a 19th century villa or a renaissance castle, innovation realization tends to take place in a "garden shed".

The positioning of innovation within a company says much about the attention paid to innovation by that company. Is the distance too large to bridge, or actually too close? Where innovation lies in relation to the head office mirrors the vision of innovation and its contribution to strategy.

The commitment to innovation, the ability to assess its yield based on added value, and the nourishment it receives from an organization reveals much about the organization's connection to innovation. Ideally, "electric cables" and "water pipes" run from the head office to the garden shed, to keep innovation healthy with strategy and value propositions from the company. Incidentally, innovation isn't just fed by the company. It can be a good idea to use alternative sources of knowledge and means on occasion, and forge alliances with other companies, knowledge institutes, and parties.

Developments in the field of innovation don't depend exclusively on location and connection; the structure is equally important. As befitting a garden shed, this structure should be simple, manageable and functional, and the innovation team working in the garden shed should have access to high-quality and process-linked connections to the various divisions of the organization. After all, innovation needs processes, maybe even more so than creativity. These processes provide answers to essential questions about the innovation team's work from the beginning (Who will be included in the innovation team? How will we manage this as a project?), to the middle on to the end (What are the right decision moments? How can we incorporate the results of earlier innovations into our process?). This is how an idea can become a winner.

Innovation is not focused on a single success, but on a thousand and one ideas. Some die an early death, being unattainable or not innovative enough, while others lead to a first concept, a prototype or model. The intermediate steps must not only be assessed by the innovation team, but must leave the garden shed and be delivered to the main office. The company should ask itself if the innovation is truly desired, and what the market demands. It should consider how the innovation aligns to company strategy and what value it adds to business. It should think about what is needed to turn this in-between idea into a success. These questions should be asked at every stop/go stage of the innovation, after which the innovation team can return to their garden shed to prepare the next step.

As innovation forms the main part of my work, I can occasionally be found in a garden shed, like I was during a recent project on the using a water system as an energy buffer. The other members of the team came from various parts of the organization, and together we did our best to turn the concept in our garden shed into a success. Following the initial feasibility scan, we concentrated particularly on the processes involved in aligning our innovation with strategy, the added value, and maintaining support. I hope it will be a success, but until then the team and I continue to work on other innovative processes that move us forward.

Glenn Bijvoets is Innovation Officer at Eneco, and is fascinated by the value of knowledge.

Innovation in Management

Julian Birkinshaw

What is the future of management? If you keep even half an eye on the business press, you'll have noticed commentators predicting dramatic changes ahead. Some foresee a virtual world where we're all freelancers selling our services to the highest bidder, often working remotely without ever meeting our clients. Others see the demise of traditional top-down management and the emergence of an empowered, motivated and self-organized workforce.

It's easy to get caught up in this way of thinking. We see the massive changes underway in technology and connectivity, and assume that these changes will also modify how we work. The trouble is...we have been here before. In the late 1990s, commentators saw us entering the *ICE* age, where *ICE* was an acronym for "the Internet Changes Everything". In the early 1980s, the business world was abuzz with talk of employee empowerment, and with the idea that computers would herald the end of middle management. Go back further still, to the 1960s or 1930s, and it's the same story—the bad, old, machine-like organizations of the past are being overthrown and replaced with enlightened and humane companies that put their employees first.

Here's the puzzle: every generation predicts that the nature of management work is changing before our eyes, and that the future will be more democratic, flat and employee-centric. Every generation has evidence that the emerging model is better. But while some things do indeed change (for example: the use of IT systems for managing our business process, the offshoring and outsourcing of work, the cycle-time for new product development), the vast majority of management work—by which I mean how we motivate people, make decisions, set objectives and allocate resources—seems almost impervious to change.

Why is this the case? Remember, we have pretty solid evidence that companies who put their employees first outperform others over a long-term period. Yet despite the conscious efforts of some management innovators (and many commentators), we are still stuck with an industrial-revolution era approach to management built on concepts like hierarchy, bureaucracy, planning and control.

I see four interlinked reasons for this:

- The traditional model of management is so pervasive that it's still the safe way of doing things. No one ever got fired for hiring IBM, or for using an enterprise resource planning system. Equally, there aren't enough alternative role models out there to give inspiration to those wanting to do things differently.

- The traditional model also has an explicit power structure that makes life very comfortable for those at the top of the tree. It's a rare individual who willingly gives up power—ask Hosni Mubarak—so the hierarchy-oriented status quo persists.

- New approaches to management are initially pretty fragile. They require people to work in ways that are unfamiliar, they require more skill, and they need different types of incentive. Often they work fine on a temporary basis, but once problems arise—a recession, a change in personnel, a new set of regulations—those who are responsible revert to type and pull control back to the center.

- Many of the old model's problems are so systemic that it's impossible for even a large company to challenge them. Everyone agrees that banking bonuses are out of line, but if one bank changes its approach unilaterally, its best people will be quickly lost to its competitors. System-wide change is needed, but we the collaborative bodies to make such change happen is lacking.

So what does the future look like? Well, the good news is that we're starting to see some new role models, thanks to the interactive, community-based version of the Internet called Web 2.0. The likes of Linux, Mozilla, Google,

Amazon, and eBay all grew up in an online world, with a majority of Gen Y employees. As a result, they're managed in a far more enlightened way than their traditional competition, providing inspiration to others.

But in all honesty, these new methods are not going to transform the BPs, the Toyotas and the General Electrics of this world. Rather, they provide insights that let traditional companies capture some of the benefits of the "new economy" without sacrificing the benefits of scale, efficiency and control that their "old economy" models currently offer. I believe smart management is about making conscious choices—when to use top-down decision-making, and when to use the collective wisdom of my employees—rather than following the crowd. When armed with a good understanding of both the old and the new worlds, executives are better positioned to make those choices.

Julian Birkinshaw, *London Business School, www.reinventingmanagement.com*

Open Innovation at Work

Jo de Boeck, Jaap Lombaers

A well-defined, focused research domain is essential to any open innovation partnership that aims to have an international position. The domain should address the research needs of an industry for the next 5-10 years, with an emphasis on applied research. A good understanding of the R&D competition brings global awareness of how to "make the difference" and create a unique technology position in the selected domain.

Holst Centre is an "Open Innovation" research centre executing "Shared Research Programs". The 35 participating companies truly form a diverse ecosystem, from SME to multinational and from equipment manufacturers and material suppliers to end-product manufacturers. They consider each other's participation as added value for the program, and often are each other's potential suppliers and customers in a value chain.

The most important asset of the centre is its talent. From the start, HR efforts have aimed at bringing in excellence and diversity, with a good mix of academic and industrial experience and enthusiastic graduates fresh from their BSc, MSc or PhD degree. Prior to their employment, the latter often receive training at the centre during their studies. Holst Centre's talent includes 30 nationalities, reflecting the international profile of its partnership.

Having a well thought out process for contracting partners and handling intellectual property is essential to success. The way of formalizing partnerships has been adapted from Interuniversity Microelectronics Centre (imec) to the specifics of research domains. As consortium agreements are rather inflexible and more suited to a project-oriented collaboration, the centre has bilateral agreements with each of the partners. The combination of these bilateral agreements sets the scene for shared research. Holst Centre is responsible for coherence of the contracts and the partnerships. Participants pay a substantial yearly participation fee and consider the centre as an extension to their R&D.

Other factors contributing to the success of the centre are immediate access to shared facilities and a dynamic region location. Philips decided to enable third-party use of many of its highly qualified research labs and facilities on the High-Tech Campus Eindhoven. This allowed the centre to immediately start research activities in 2006 without having to make initial significant investments. Complementary to that, the centre has itself made investments that tackle new routes of technology development.

Enthusiasm and the spirit of doing something special in a pioneering atmosphere is essential to all this. TNO and imec provided Holst Centre's management with significant autonomy to reinvent processes of innovation and experiment with new flavors of open innovation partnership. Full-time seniors in management and R&D with excellent qualifications were dedicated to the setup and success of the centre from day one. Re-inventing the organization and reviewing the progress research portfolio frequently have maintained both this pioneering spirit and the growth of the centre's impact.

Jo de Boeck and Jaap Lombaers, Holst Centre

Innovation Delivery in Animal Health

Ellen de Brabander

The animal health market segment has a market size of about $20 billion. Companies active in this segment develop, manufacture, and commercialize pharmaceutical products and vaccines for production animals (cattle, swine, poultry, fish) and/or companion animals (dogs, cats, horses) in order to both enhance the animals' health and well being, and feed the world. There's a strong need for new and improved products in this market, which is driven by emerging diseases (e.g. Bluetongue virus in sheep, West Nile virus in horses, Circovirus in swine) or unmet needs (e.g. cancer in companion animals). Additionally, societal or regulatory demands may dictate the need to develop new products (salmonella vaccines for chicken) or to use resources in different ways than in the past. Meeting these needs is now increasingly possible thanks to better insight and the rapid development of technologies needed to develop new and improved products.

Animal health is a highly regulated industry with an approval process similar to that of human pharma products: before a product is approved its safety, efficacy, and consistent manufacturability must be demonstrated. In general, each of the target animal species has its own health needs for products, which often differ from region to region.

One of the positive features of developing new products for animal health is the relatively high probability of success once a product enters the development stage. This high success probability is mainly due to the fact that in an earlier research phase new candidate products have been tested in the target animal to define proof of concept or to understand the mode of action. Also for a number of main indications, such as anti-parasitics, clinical model and field trial end points may be the same well-defined process.

Because of species diversity and a broad range of needs, portfolio management is key in animal health—which animal species most need a new product and what should the target product profile be (i.e., what is the balance between the ideal product profile, the resources and time needed and POS to achieve this profile)? It's important to ensure a balanced pipeline that is in line with company strategy: balancing the animal species and geographic regions, development stages, and the riskportfolio. Clearly, this step requires input from commercial marketing, manufacturing, and all the R&D departments.

The second step is about excellence in execution: getting organized, allocating resources to the highest priority projects, having the right quality people available, and delivering the projects in line with the agreed upon plan. This step, though it sounds simple, has proven to be a real challenge.

In order to achieve registration of a new product a multi-year (up to a decade), multi-functional, and multi-site project must be successfully realized. Project teams in animal health tend to be relatively small and operate in complex, dynamic, and competitive environments. Therefore, project management and functional excellence are key pillars for success. Project teams generally have only one representative per function, so it is critical that this person is not only an expert in his/her function (regulatory affairs, for example) but also be able to communicate his/her expertise to project team members who specialize in other areas.

By applying these principles within Merial R&D, we've been able to increase the pipeline value by more than 50%, advance high priority pipeline projects in line with planning, increase confidence in the innovation engine, and boost morale—success is one of the most effective motivators in professional life.

Ellen de Brabander is Chief Scientific Officer at Merial Limited and Governing Board Member of EIT. eit.europa.eu

Starting Fires

Marcelo Bravo

I'm an entrepreneur...I guess. When people ask, "What is it that you do?" I still have trouble answering. I do many different things and the word "entrepreneur" simply fails to capture that. "I am an entrepreneur" is a good enough answer for the sake of simplicity, but I go on to explain in broad brushstrokes what I've been doing for the past eight years since I left the corporate world. I've been a company founder, an angel investor, a public company CEO, a deal maker, a fundraiser, businessman, and more. I have started or been part of four startups, two of which I've taken public, one which has gone into liquidation and one that's only just starting. I have had moments of great personal difficulty. I've had a company skyrocket in the stock market—then crash. Now I'm doing fine, and am comfortable and skilled at navigating turbulent and uncertain waters. Most importantly, I'm happy doing what I'm best at—starting companies from scratch.

I'm interested in companies anchored in science or technology, light in organizational structure and physical assets but capable of scaling globally at a fast pace. I prefer companies that can have an impact in the world and make life better. I'm also interested in stuff that makes me tick, that I can understand and affect.

Starting and growing these companies is like starting a fire. Long ago as a boy scout, I learned the highly skilled craft of starting a fire from scratch. You need three elements to start and grow a fire: fuel, oxygen and heat. If any of these elements are removed the fire dies. To start and grow a fire you need to dose and balance these three ingredients delicately and skillfully.

It's the same with startup companies, but your three key elements are ideas, people and money.

You can have the greatest idea in the world but without people to realize it or the financial resources to make it happen, your idea will never manifest. Good ideas are like dry twigs that light easily and help start your fire. Bad ideas are green or wet branches that won't light. A dry branch that is too large to light with your little match is also a bad idea.

People are essential, as we all know. They are your oxygen. The right people will make a bad idea succeed and likewise the wrong people will screw up the greatest concept. VC's often say they invest in teams, not ideas. Entrepreneurs are not always best equipped to realize their idea, but it's vital for would-be entrepreneurs to understand where they fit in the picture and how their role may need to change as the fire grows.

There is a basic law of money in startups: you always need more than you think you need, and that's usually a lot. Money presents entrepreneurs with a paradox. I'd argue that money is the only commodity amongst the three ingredients, yet it's often the scarcest of the three. There's more money that anyone can imagine zipping around the world looking eagerly for returns; it's the entrepreneur's job to understand and master the art of tapping into it.

Awareness of the three basic elements of entrepreneurship is merely the first step in the art and craft of starting and growing companies. Like any other art and craft there's a great deal of technique and know-how to learn, and the only way to truly master it is through practice.

Get out there and start a fire!

Marcelo Bravo is Founder and Chief Technology Officer at Oxford Pharmascience Group Plc.

Success Depends on How Clearly You Hear Your Customers

Christina Hepner Brodie

Voice of the Customer (VoC) methodologies have significantly improved the design of innumerable products since entering the managerial mainstream in the early 1990s. A growing number of companies are gathering first-hand input from their customers and applying it to their product development decisions and processes, obtaining a decided competitive advantage in exchange for their efforts. Few enterprises currently apply comparable VoC information to other aspects of their broader business and operational strategies, however. For firms prepared to overcome the internal hurdles to applying VoC techniques in this wider context, the return on investment promises to be considerable.

The Internet has provided the business world with a compelling reason to ground a wider range of decisions in VoC learning. Although the use of this channel is a given, not every company understands just how to use the Internet to maximize its benefits to both the company and its customers. The optimal use of electronic linking capabilities that enable companies to directly interface with their suppliers and customers is best achieved by first determining what specific needs are served by creating such links. By using VoC research to understand the dynamics at play in electronic linking technologies, thoughtful leaders with deep experience in their company and industry can drive the use of electronic solutions, rather than being driven by those with electronic solutions to sell.

Certain business leaders are especially adept at discerning what customers need—by listening to them. This isn't some intuitive gift; it comes either from drawing deeply from the reservoir of customer and market knowledge naturally formed through years of experience in an industry, or from long experience in developing strategies, products, or services for a particular market or customer set. When managers with deep enough institutional memory and experience draw on those resources to identify customers who can provide the most powerful and useful insights, and then personally interview those customers, they create a context in which they can see, hear, and learn for the good of their companies.

Leaps of insight generally result from executives who enter the process with a genuine openness to intuition and discovery, not a predisposition to confirm their own hypotheses. As the mathematician Jules Henri Poincaré noted, "It is by logic that we prove, but by intuition that we discover." It's important to understand that customers' voices are only one input to VoC discovery. Transmuting customer input into business solutions calls for informed intelligence and sensing ability on the part of the interviewers as well as those who analyze, assess, and ultimately understand the interview transcripts.

The phrase "Voice of the Customer" has sometimes been taken to imply that your customers make your decisions for you. Yet a customer-driven organization has lost its leadership when it lapses into being customer-led. Blindly acting on customer input is a recipe for disaster. It can send a company scurrying to satisfy the demands of a handful of sample customers who don't reflect the company's larger market. It can also lead a company to develop strategies that address today's customer issues—not tomorrow's. The potential richness of VoC data is lost when applied literally, narrowly, or passively.

The ultimate value of the VoC is derived not from capturing collections of verbatim "voices", but from the rigorous analysis and interpretation that follow. Using language processing tools such as Center for Quality of Management's Language Processing Method® and Method for Priority Marking® facilitates a common understanding of customer input. VoC tools work not because they're silver bullets, but because they channel the VoC team's knowledge and experience through the discipline of formal process. Of course, if a VoC project is relegated to personnel with little experience or knowledge, the results will contain decidedly limited insight and value, no matter how closely tested VoC methodologies are adhered to. Effective language-processing tools enhance the value of qualitative VoC data by aligning the thinking and decision-making of those involved.

CEOs need to conduct customer engagement themselves if they want their innovation strategies to be informed with a customer perspective. Of course, the predictable reaction of many executives and senior managers is that they don't have time to conduct interviews or "process data." Yet it is precisely these senior people who are most able to understand the context of interviewees' remarks and make intuitive connections between the VoC data and business opportunities. Executives who are new to a company, or especially an industry, can benefit enormously from participating in VoC projects with their more seasoned colleagues. It's an excellent way for a new executive to quickly become grounded in the issues facing their customers, and thus their companies.

The success of your business and its strategy development depends on how clearly you can hear your customers.

Christina Hepner Brodie is co-author of Voices into Choices: Acting on the Voice of the Customer, *and Lead Principal of PwC/PRTM, based in Waltham, Massachusetts, USA. www.prtm.com, www.pwc.com/us*

How Manufacturers and Retailers Can Partner for Profit

Mick Broekhof

Today's industry leaders compete to win with open innovation, working with various partners in the value chain (including universities and companies from other industries) by opening up to external partnerships, increasing reliance on collaborative idea generation and becoming less protective of intellectual property. As a result, successful open innovation partnerships enable new and meaningful ways to satisfy both customer and consumer, building bottom line results for all value chain partners.

Collaborative innovation is an open innovation strategy that enables consumer packaged goods (CPG) manufacturers and retailers to partner for profit and provide shoppers and consumers with more innovative offerings.

What's Working for CPG

Today's manufacturers and retailers each face significant, but different, challenges. Despite different business imperatives, there's common ground that drives collaboration. The value of collaborating is clear: manufacturers and retailers are gaining an increase in sales and profits, and blockbuster results, by jointly growing the category. In fact, there's potential for a 15-20% sales and profit improvement opportunity—blockbuster territory.

By working together, manufacturers and retailers can develop better promotion vehicles, enhance in-store support, and develop unique, value-added offerings for both the retailer and the manufacturer.

Other benefits include:

- Improving idea generation

- Incorporating shopper and consumer insight data to make better decisions

- Reducing rework

- Increasing speed to market

- Improving execution

What Isn't Working for CPG
While many companies are claiming to collaboratively innovate, the right initiatives aren't in place and the right due diligence is often lacking. The result is innovation that isn't working to an organization's full advantage.

While the urgency and need for collaborative innovation is clear, questions remain:

- How does an organization know if they are implementing it correctly?

- How do they know where it fits into their business model?

- How do they make sure it is working most efficiently for them?

Conclusions
Manufacturers and retailers that engage in a true collaborative innovation approach achieve more innovation, enhanced shop-ability, and better alignment. From a profitability perspective, they jointly achieve higher revenue coupled with reduced costs for developing profitable business. The potential benefits are tremendous. However, many companies are only achieving pockets of success. Companies know they need—and want—collaborative innovation, but don't know exactly how to do it.

How to Get Started
We recommend an approach that can broadly and systemically deploy collaborative innovation within an organization by following four best practices:

- Develop a strategy for collaborative innovation

- Conduct collaborative business planning

- Get your house in order

- Build trusted relationships

Mick Broekhof is a Founding Partner and Head of the CPG Practice of Kalypso. He has over 30 years experience in global corporate management and consulting. www.kalypso.com

Designing a "Fast Innovation" Delivery Back-End

Nicolas Bry

Having a "rapid innovation" engine is a must-have in a competitive market where competitors come in from other parts of the world and from other industries with shorter development cycles, and where customers are difficult to seduce. Innovation is key for differentiation, and it has to be done quickly since the second version is often the right one! Speed is an essential part of the innovation process. To quote the Google innovation team, "The faster we are, the better we become."

According to Vijay Govindarajan, "Innovation cannot happen inside the performance engine, it requires a dedicated innovation team, essentially creating a startup company."

At Orange, a large mobile and fixed international carrier issued from France Telecom, we set up an innovation entity called New Co acting as a startup. New Co was created to identify, develop, and market innovative products and services within particularly short lead times, complementing the Group's digital portfolio.

The adventure has been running for three years now, and the following lessons have been learned:

- New Co succeeded in identifying many "hot topics" like music-on-demand or smart TV, developing prototypes and performing market tests: the mission as a scout and a "house for ideas" has been accomplished.

- New Co has developed and launched a diversified range of products outside of the traditional carrier's boundaries: from a tactile tablet, a mobile address book app, and a photo web application for family memories to an open transmedia lab designing multiplatform apps.

- It's been harder to achieve streamlined cooperation with the core company, facilitating further product inclusion in the Group portfolio.

- We haven't been very forward thinking in terms of building effective innovation management; the portfolio doesn't have a balance of disruption and quick wins, and its intent is rather ambiguous. There's no innovation process pairing "open innovation" with "design thinking," and our own know-how, nor is there encouragement for cross-team sharing.

Learning from both our experiences and in-depth reviews of academic sources and 15 case studies, I suggested an optimized architecture—the *Rapid Innovation* model—based on three pillars:

- A dedicated entity that would leverage on its agility and autonomy, and simultaneously be half cast, mapping part of its portfolio with core co-expectations, in the form of quick wins

- Creative tension as an acceleration trigger for development, with key components that include a culture of diversity, openness to opportunities picked out from the "innovation market", focus, tight goals, and knowledge circulation

- Innovation strategy alignment that forges persistent connections with mainstream operations, cultivates communication and borrows skills from the core company, forming teams that engage the core company and create a line of least resistance

Can this happen in a week? Of course not! We suggest a rapid innovation plan over a nine-month timeline over three main stages—Create, Develop, Engage.

Haste is one thing; speed is another. Setting up a speedy back-end doesn't alleviate the need for innovation design that emotionally engages our customers with a combination of feasibility, usability and desirability.

Nicolas Bry is Senior VP at Orange Innovation, with experience in developing digital innovation. He wrote a thesis on rapid innovation at HEC Business School. nbry.wordpress.com

Principles for Building an Entrepreneurial National Ecosystem

Will Cardwell

In organizing the Aalto University Center for Entrepreneurship, which is among the first to combine technology transfer, initialization services for academic startups, and support for entrepreneurial learning and research programs, we've tried to reduce the complex and chaotic challenges of growth company creation into a few simple principles. Finland, like most other economies, needs high-growth firms to emerge in order to support the intergenerational financial crisis that virtually all Western countries face over the next 25 years, unless fundamental changes take place. Many of us feel that a new culture in better alignment with market needs—one that embraces risk and celebrates both failure and success—must arise.

I believe that a great entrepreneurial ecosystem can be summarized by the following fundamental principles:

- Recognizing where "unfair" competitive advantages exist in an economy

- Creating and nurturing an extreme work-ethic around those competitive advantages

- Enabling the flexibility necessary to benefit from unpredictable market movements

I'll use Finland as an example, but I think most countries can identify similar cultural attributes. In a way, Finland has an oversupply of "unfair" advantage. Its infrastructure and primary education are among the best in the world, which has led to fantastic (and well-documented) know-how in a variety of sectors. This is due to solid economic principles and years of focus on the need for societal innovation. However, the other two principles face huge challenges.

Extreme work, to me, means enabling and supporting the best entrepreneurs in their highly intense, well-connected work. This 24/7 environment means that people work far longer than a conventional working week over significant "sprint" periods, which definitely takes its toll over time. Public policy must recognize that entrepreneurs who target high growth are a specialized group who need both disproportionate benefits when theysucceed, and fast recovery when they fail. This calls for a progressive tax system, streamlined bankruptcy procedures and encouragement of unconventional wellness services that cater to a 24/7 lifestyle. Malcolm Gladwell's *Outliers* is a great reference book for identifying how to achieve excellence; I encourage all entrepreneurs and policymakers to read it.

Market windows open for an innovation when least expected, so flexibility is crucial. An entrepreneur must move quickly, whether sooner or later than planned. Building both funding instruments and board governance principles for startups is critical at this juncture. U.S. venture capitalists have shown their genius in that their boards are set up to be agile and handle risk—when the market window opens, external funders are immediately prepared to deviate from the plan and ramp up the funding. Nicholas Taleb's *The Black Swan* is my favorite reference for this.

These 3 principles aren't rocket science. But I think most potential policy recommendations have room to improve at least one of those categories. While building sustainable national competitive advantage is a long-term theme, focusing on the other two can also bring short-term satisfaction.

Will Cardwell, *Aalto University Center for Entrepreneurship, Finland*

Building and Managing a Team

Nick Case

Many people have bright ideas for a new product or service, but most of those ideas remain exactly that—an idea. The failure rate is high for those that make it to the prototype stage. Ideas that make it to production have a reasonable survival rate, but major successes are few and far between.

One of the main challenges faced by any early stage business is creating a team that can take the business through all the various growth stages. At each stage, different skills will be needed; it's a rare entrepreneur who combines all of the required skill sets.

The biggest obstacle to circumventing the problem is getting founders or owners to recognize this fact. Many small businesses are forever doomed to remain small because the founders or owners simply won't accept their own limitations. Even if they *do* come round to this realization, they often can't bring themselves to do two things that are crucial if the business is to grow and thrive.

Delegating responsibility is the first requirement—and the more vital of the two. Put simply, the founders/owners must learn to believe that somebody else is as well (and quite likely better) qualified to take on certain responsibilities. Many early stage businesses never progress beyond the "promising" stage because the founders/owners need to make every decision, however miniscule.

Secondly, the founders/owners must at least consider the possibility of giving up control of the business they have been building. No matter how often the mantra "better a small shareholder in a large business than a large shareholder in a small business" is mentioned, for many the message just never gets through.

Once the founders/owners have taken the first (and ideally the second) of these two steps, it'll be easier to move the process on to the next logical stage, which is to recognize that a team can never remain static if a business is to become truly successful. The ultimate aim should be to hire a team of people each of whom is better than the founder in their specific roles.

Nick Case, *2degrees*

Implant Success for the Future

Claudia Cavaleiro

We recently developed and introduced a product using completely new processing technology, making our products more sustainable. It was a complete novelty in the food world—taking an existing core product and modifying it without changing either taste or texture. For the most successful implementation, we designed in advance and looked at prerequisites in order to avoid any issues.

The biggest challenge for our innovation process was going from trials to production line without knowing exactly, how our product would perform. The second largest challenge, which appeared more often, was intermediate scope changes. Everything had to be right first time, from consumer satisfaction to efficient production. For these challenges, our innovation process in combination with Design for Six Sigma was most supportive.

Collaboration was of key importance. The process passed through three different teams before it hit the factory: Future Science and Technology, Product Innovation, and Product and Process Implementation. We partnered with a university to develop new ingredients and technology, and we applied a highly structured scientific tool method including Design for Six Sigma. We also ensured that all the expert teams were in sync and willing to try a structured and rigorous new approach, concentrating on consumer demand. The willingness to collaborate made for a very efficient process.

We used the Six Sigma Tool, which definitely streamlined the process. Six Sigma is closely connected to lean and has 99 tools (including many lean tools), a data-based process that works with a scientific decision framework, and a structure with consumer-based lean processes.

The results were encouraging: fast commissioning, a high-quality product first off the production line, and excellent initial line performance.

We've learned that a structured Stage-Gate® Process in combination with Design for Six Sigma will bring success to new product and process development.

You have to really push to bring an innovative product to life, yet also carefully balance effort and value with the probability of success. Always go back and check against product development with R&D and Marketing, to make sure that the product is fully developed in terms of quality and efficiency. Learn to deal in facts, taking a fresh look and a step back during the innovation process, and keep asking if what you're doing makes sense. Ultimately, to be successful your delivery must focus on the voice of the consumer.

Claudia Cavaleiro, *Mars*

Bringing New Ideas to Market: The Collaboration Imperative

Beth Comstock

Do the best ideas always win? If only they did! In large organizations, great ideas can unfortunately get lost in a sea of other great ideas, or tread water due to lack of focus, intolerance of ambiguity, or fear of failure. In smaller organizations and startups, you can be single-minded in purpose and take on risk, but the resources to grow great ideas into their fullest potential aren't always there. It's all too common to have an amazing idea, dedicate time, funding and patience to development and testing, it and— Eureka! You prove the concept, but it still doesn't scale. Inspiration, passion and diligence are essential to keep an idea going...but sometimes you need help getting out of your own way. Short of summoning a superhero, what's an innovator to do?

The key may lie outside your organization's four walls. By connecting with other innovators and partners in an open, transparent manner, you can tap into all kinds of power—often where you least expect to find it.

At GE, we're learning this lesson through partnerships that range from startup joint ventures to open calls for action. Take our recent $200 million ecomagination Challenge, which brought together bright minds and 5,000 business ideas from 150 countries to tackle the world's energy problems. We recognized that good ideas come from everywhere, but underestimated the enormous might that also comes from something a company of our size knows well—the ability to scale and to get a wide range of ideas to market. A commercially viable idea requires interaction and commitment between entrepreneurs, innovators, funders and partners. In some ways, the money's the easy part. Based on the Challenge, we recently created an internal cleantech acceleration group whose mission is to ensure the ideas we're funding scale faster with the help of GE's operational, marketing and selling expertise.

We also learned about the power of community. Sure, these crowds are wise, but they're also vibrant, vocal and demand accountability. The eco Challenge community—75,000 people strong—helped sharpen our decision making, questioned the status quo and optimized each other's chances for commercial success in a global energy market. The community became its own matchmaker for startups, seeing connection points others hadn't.

We know innovation can originate from anywhere at anytime. To compete in the global marketplace, companies like GE need an approach to innovation that supports open collaboration and partnership—especially when dealing with big world challenges like the environment or healthcare, which are too complicated for any one entity to solve alone.

Five years after launching our business initiative ecomagination, we learned that innovation works best when everyone in the ecosystem participates— big companies, small companies, entrepreneurs, local government, the public sector, and individuals. Cooperation is key. Our customers want that too, since they also benefit from a network of ideas and capabilities. Working with more partners has further convinced us that collaboration is the fastest, most effective way to bring about change. Together, we're smarter, savvier, stronger, and a lot more innovative too. While this doesn't mean *every* great idea will get off the ground, there's one thing we're sure of—we can do great things with a little help from our friends.

Beth Comstock, SVP and Chief Marketing Officer of GE, leads the company's global innovation strategy, which includes the business initiatives ecomagination and healthymagination. www.ge.com

Delivery Challenges in Networked Innovation: Early Involvement and a Shared Language

Fleur Deken

Nowadays many products require a range of knowledge and technical capabilities that a single company may not possess. Companies increasingly often join forces in networks to enhance their innovation potential. I studied the development of the Senseo, which was the collaborative result of a larger network of companies with Sara Lee and Philips as main partners.

In the Senseo case, the diverse knowledge bases of the various companies had to be integrated into a single product. For instance, Sara Lee had the expertise on what constitutes a good cup of coffee, and Philips understood technical design for mass production. These diverse knowledge bases enabled the creation of a new coffee maker concept.

From studying the collaboration process, I found two reasons why managing the process in an innovation network could be particularly complex: the temporal membership of companies in the network and the diversity of work processes and knowledge.

Since you never know for sure where an innovation project will lead to, it is often impossible to determine all the necessary knowledge upfront. Some companies in the Senseo case were involved during the opportunity identification phase and some during the early product conceptualization, whereas others only participated during the innovation delivery stage. When companies left the network, they took their knowledge with them— obviously, they didn't bring it into the network until they were part of it, though it could've been useful at an earlier stage. For instance Philips entered a bit later, but their input would have come in handy during several early design decisions, which could have smoothed out the innovation delivery process.

Another challenge was achieving common understanding and coordinating interdependent tasks across organizational boundaries. What Sara Lee called a "prototype", for example, was a "feasibility study" for Philips. As a former product manager from Philips explained in relation to the innovation delivery phase, "Sara Lee was not used to working with those sorts of milestones. You have to convince them that such tests are really necessary. It takes a lot of energy to explain to each other what your processes are exactly, and what the conventions are when managing a project. You look from a very different perspective to such [innovation] processes." As such, innovation networks need constant coordination throughout all the process stages, rather than division of remits made in the early innovation stage based on a fragile common understanding informed by incomplete knowledge.

Although there are large potential gains from participating in them, innovation networks are no magic bullet. The greater the diversity between the organizations in the network, the greater the opportunities are for tapping into new knowledge bases and enhancing innovation potential. Yet, at the same time, the challenges are greater. Coordination challenges may be especially fierce in the innovation delivery phases, where everything must fall into place.

Coffee has been a sturdy business for centuries, where margins slowly deteriorated. Now intensive network coordination is stirring up a revolution with more coffee enjoyment, more business growth and more profit.

Fleur Deken is a PhD Researcher on Networked Innovation at the Delft University of Technology.

Give Yourself a SWOT

Luke Disney

Before you set out on the path from the drawing board to the boardroom, take a good long look in the mirror. At the very least you'll save yourself some grey hair; at most you just might save your innovation.

When I took the reins of North Star Alliance in 2007, I inherited the responsibility of taking a simple but powerful innovation in healthcare and turning it into a public-private partnership that would save lives across sub-Saharan Africa. The concept of building networked chains of roadside health clinics to reach mobile populations that were both suffering from and transmitting high-impact diseases like HIV, malaria and tuberculosis was someone else's idea—my job was to make it happen.

But before getting started I had to clear one small hurdle: I didn't have a background in healthcare or building distribution networks. I needed allies—and, eventually, colleagues—to help me get the job done. I was never under the illusion that I had all the answers. In fact, sometimes it seemed like all I had were questions!

Thankfully, there's an entire industry out there called consulting, which does nothing but provide answers to questions (with the added benefit that consultants are relatively easy to part company with if they don't have the answers you need). There comes a time in your organizational development, however, when you need *more* than a consultant. You need a team: a well-oiled machine with all the right parts, working in harmony towards a common goal. The first steps you take in building your machine are by far the most important, as a poor choice at the beginning will impact on all the choices made afterwards.

When I started building the North Star team, I took a good long look in the mirror. What was I good at? What was I not so good at? What type of people could I work with? What could I compromise on, and which aspects of my working style were set in stone? Based on what I saw in my reflection, I made the first choices for my team. They weren't always obvious choices, and not necessarily people I would have chosen to work with under other conditions. However, they were the right choices for the job at hand. By taking a look in the mirror and giving myself a good SWOT (strengths, weaknesses, opportunities, threats), I brought together a team that took the innovation of healthcare for mobile populations and turned it into a network of 22 roadside wellness centers in 10 countries in under five years.

A SWOT analysis is a tried and tested business tool. When you need to build a team that will turn your "Eureka!" into Eureka Inc., take a look in the mirror and give yourself a good SWOT. It might be a little uncomfortable, but the results are well worth it.

Luke Disney is Executive Director of North Star Alliance, a public-private partnership providing mobile populations in Africa with access to healthcare. www.northstar-alliance.org

Innovation: A Return to Reality

Michel ten Donkelaar, Richard Bordenave

Many fast-moving consumer goods companies (FMCGs) follow new product development processes to bring new product ideas to market. Typically, these processes consist of a series of stages with critical gates to prioritize projects; this helps management optimize resources and filter out projects before too much money is spent. Generally, teams have to jump various hurdles to convince senior management to allocate R&D and marketing resources so they can proceed, step by step, from idea to launch. This "design" journey is a Darwinian path, along which project teams face the harsh realities of technological constraints and P&L targets while trying to bring their ideas to life for consumers. Many projects lead to dead ends as a result of cost, volume or pricing issues. The survivors face a final test— the moment of truth (MOT) with the consumer, hopefully prior to launch. The 1st MOT is when the shopper is exposed to the new product; the 2nd MOT is when the consumer uses it.

The paradox is that validation of 1st and 2nd MOTs most frequently takes place in the later stages of the NPD process, when most development spending has already been committed. Unfavorable conclusions then jeopardize the entire project. The way back is difficult: R&D expenses have reached their peaks, product specifications are frozen, and marketers are both over-committed to trade and determined not to miss the launch window. There are only two ways out of this problem: either a costly rework, resulting in longer time to market and increased R&D investment, or the launch of a flawed mix. The impact on P&L is disastrous in both cases. Shocking innovation mortality statistics confirm that this situation is more the rule than the exception.

A new approach to innovation, called "design thinking", challenges the traditional linear approach. Most NPD processes adopt linear thinking for resource management purposes, which is fine but highly questionable when applied to the research sequence. Shopper or user context has a disproportionate influence on innovation performance for FMCGs. It's surprising to note that this is still ignored in most research methodologies that test concepts without considering competitive environment, or survey consumers who might show interest in the idea but never actually visit the aisle in which the product will be sold.

The general assumption behind these methods is that ideas or concepts should be evaluated first, and design work is about finding a way to deliver these ideas. In-store performance now appears to be the ultimate lever to apply at the end of process. But in an FMCG, reality doesn't work like this. Consumers buy and experience "product executions", not concepts or strategies. In-store activation doesn't compensate in the long term for flawed innovation design. This linear thinking is problematic when dealing with the research sequence because it relies in the early stages on consumer feedback, from stimuli using words or images, while we now know that shopper behavior is influenced by many unconscious factors such as sensory information, emotions, habits and a competitive environment. As a consequence, marketing teams often have unrealistic expectations of research, assuming, for example, that they can derive a sales forecast from a ten-line concept or a few screen clicks.

"Design thinking" reverses the research approach, trying to build execution into strategy and dealing with reality. "Designers" use rough touch-and-feel prototypes in the very early stages to help consumers experience and explore their ideas in real environments and reveal latent optimizations that can't be spotted on a concept board—the best insights come from store aisles or a real usage context. Including 1st & 2nd MOT early on helps change product definition at a stage when it still has minimal impact on costs. It also allows for improvements to product specifications delivering more consumer satisfaction.

Merging shopper and user insights is the preferred route: a first step to a better understanding of the consumer as a whole person engaged in an everyday activity, like shopping or eating. This realistic approach also reduces the risk of discovering inconsistent results between what consumers claim in the early stages and what shoppers actually do in store, or users do at home.

Michel ten Donkelaar is the Consumer Insights Director for Kraft Biscuits Europe, and Market Researcher of the Year 2011 in the Netherlands.
Richard Bordenave works with InVivo/BVA.

Innovation Processes
Are Not Projects

Patrick van der Duin

I often present my students with a choice of two client types:

- Client 1 knows exactly what he wants, how much it should cost and what the final product should look like.

- Client 2 has a vague idea of what he wants, can only estimate the costs and doesn't know how long the project will last.

A surprising amount of students opt for Client 1; that could be because I teach at a university of technology. What I want to illustrate is that "Client 1 students" are more suited to project management and "Client 2 students" concentrate best on innovation processes.

The North/South Metro Line in Amsterdam exemplifies the distinction between project and innovation processes. It has failed as a project, having hugely exceeded both its timeframe and budget. Yet as an innovation process, the North/South Line still has a chance of success. Amsterdam City Council can still potentially share in any financial profits that the contractors reap on the expertise they've developed by tunnel boring through weak ground in densely populated areas. The Council has, after all, paid huge fees to contractors who—quite wrongly—acted as if the North/South Line was a project.

It's essential to distinguish innovation processes from projects. Those who judge innovation processes by the same criteria as projects will quickly advocate stopping them; contrary to projects, an innovation process' progress is often unclear. By treating projects and innovation processes the same way, many innovation processes become prematurely stifled and the organization falls short of being truly innovative.

Innovation process methodology
The realization of a new concept, a developed product or business idea is not the same as a "normal" project. It's not a case of carrying out a project with

defined qualities within a set period and budget. Innovation is uncertain by definition. It is, after all, something new and therefore unproven.

Well-known project management methods such as *Prince 2* cannot be applied point by point to innovation projects. Normal project management deals with quality control according to pre-set specifications. The budget and timeframe are established and defined. Innovation activities are about increasing opportunities; there are no "exact" specifications. During the process, it's important to be open to suggestions that can create extra customer value. In a normal project, the key focus is scope. In innovation, the customer-defined product concept is the focus. Projects use fixed processes and documentation; innovation stands on the interaction between individuals and concerned parties. A typical project process starts with definitions being made, followed by the subject and finally the building. Project managers follow a tight regimen: plan, do, check, and then act. In contrast, innovation is more about the competence of the team (Source: Idea I do, www.ideaido.eu):

- Seeing: vision, insight and client empathy

- Connecting: working together, both internally and externally, staying open to opinion

- Doing: discovering + adapting = experimenting (in context)

Patrick van der Duin lectures in futures research and innovation management at Delft University of Technology.

From Product Innovation to Making the Difference Every Day

Madalina Dumitrescu, Marcin Lecki, Rafal Winiarz and Willemien Boot

The innovation journey for Mars Central Europe (a region stretching from Finland/the Baltic to Albania), though indirect, has led to immediate and clear improvement in the region's performance. It began with a sole focus on product innovation and, by way of a focus on innovation systems and processes, finally moved towards cultural change via "Making the Difference Every Day," which has culminated in projects that significantly contribute to our business performance.

Around 2005, after a growth turnaround in the region, the time came to truly capitalize on these growth opportunities and enter into contiguous product categories that showed a high growth potential. New products were developed and introduced in the market over a short period of time, showing the much faster innovation rate than before. The first 3 years of sales data was the measure for successful innovation.

This initial success sparked the drive for more focus on innovation. During this period, further research indicated that success required going beyond mere product innovation, and that successful FMCG companies gained more benefits from innovation where creativity was truly embedded in the whole organization.

This triggered a change in approach. 2007 saw the creation of a steering team, an innovation director was appointed, and innovation ambassadors were nominated to support the innovation process throughout every division of MCE. In terms of process and tools, the activity management process switched to an innovation process that incorporated both initial business challenges/consumer opportunities and lessons learned post-completion. Additionally, an open web platform was set up so associates could present their ideas and contribute to some "hot topic" business challenges.

On the personal side, a campaign was launched for associates to contribute to innovation. The intended future scenario was pictured as a place "where associates spontaneously and frequently identify new ideas, present them to others and collaboratively develop them to unique, consumer relevant solutions, which will enable MCE to deliver leading edge performance in a sustainable way." To monitor the innovation journey's progress, MCE began counting the number of ideas generated and how many associates came up with ideas and developments. Innovation was the watchword throughout the company.

By the second half of 2008 things seemed to be going wrong. The initial excitement was fading out, some innovation ambassadors backed off and a few leadership teams didn't formally have innovation on their agenda. Changes had to be made.

Clearly, moving towards an innovative culture doesn't just happen by focusing on systems, processes and targets; it requires more of a push from within the organization, and employees need a clear context for understanding how they can contribute to an innovative organization.

MCE shaped this context with 3 areas of focus:

- **Consumer Closeness:** in order to truly understand the consumer, proposed innovations must be consumer-driven and not company-driven

- **Collaboration with internal and external partners:** To benefit from new ideas, working with a broad group of stakeholders who can move ideas towards concrete innovations is essential

- **Make the Difference Every Day:** this is a recognition tool for associates who both come forward with ideas and implement them, bringing constant improvement for MCE—and ultimately the consumer. This company-wide process has now been implemented on a regular basis to both allow further associate innovation and to recognize those efforts when they are successfully implemented.

Now the focus areas are supported by associates who are passionate about their contributions, and don't feel limited by systems and targets. In 2011, over 1200 delivered projects were nominated for Making the Difference Every Day, which means that over 50% of MCE's associates participated in those projects! This in turn inspires yet more associates to innovate.

The associates now have a clear idea about how to contribute to an innovative culture and how innovation fits within an overall business objective. It's not about innovating for the sake of it, but about building a better business in Central Europe.

Madalina Dumitrescu, Marcin Lecki, Rafal Winiarz and Willemien Boot, Mars Central Europe, www.mars.com

Picking the Winners

Carolyn Dunning

Idea generation and selection is often a subjective process, yet deciding which ideas to progress is critical for the success of new innovations. Time and again over my 20+ year career, I have seen and read about new ideas and innovations that stalled halfway through the development cycle because the quality—and indeed, viability—of many of the ideas generated at the outset were not critically assessed and thought through.

If too many "good ideas" are pushed through a development process, then limited resources get spread too thinly. Critical issues that should have been fully resolved to ensure market success often get missed or aren't given enough focus. Really good ideas, such as those based on a strong consumer need or a technical breakthrough, become diluted by other projects selected for emotive reasons—often despite the business having few competencies and skills in the area. Perhaps the R&D Director has come up with a "great idea" or an article in the press means that something suddenly becomes "trendy".

It's also common that innovation teams become emotionally attached to their ideas. This is a major reason why many projects continue to soak up resources longer than they should have. If a clear reason to stop is discovered during the development process, then difficult decisions have to be made. Stopping a large project after several years of research, development, test marketing and high profile investment is far more difficult than starting it in the first place.

Each idea must therefore be critically and objectively assessed right from the start for its likelihood of success using a constructive and proven methodology. It should then be monitored throughout the process as required. Although information and data will be approximate until the later stages of development, filtering an idea using critically important factors learned from experience with innovations will greatly improve the selection of winning ideas and their chances of succeeding in the market place.

At OpenTo, we have developed such a selection filter based on our experiences of critical success criteria gleaned from many innovation projects we have been involved in over the last 20 years. Implementing such a tool will sort and prioritize new ideas and help make objective decisions as to which projects need more focus and which should be stopped.

First, critical information on the project is entered online. Feedback is then collected from nominated senior managers through an online questionnaire against which our engine then automatically generates a Likelihood of Success (LOS) ranking for each idea. The output is a set of charts that plot ideas against each other. These identify strong and weak areas for each idea and make a "Go" or "No Go" recommendation. Further analysis can be done if required.

The tool does not take the place of quantitative consumer research but rather provides a comprehensive multifunctional model looking at strategic, supply, consumer and market critical factors. Questions are included on factors that we have found often get missed yet are critical in a likelihood of success ranking.

So, ensuring your innovation pipeline consists mainly of ideas with a high LOS will increase your successes in the marketplace and improve your corporate return on innovation investment. And, the more successes you have, the greater the motivation and credibility of your business leaders and your innovation teams.

Carolyn Dunning is an Innovation Consultant at OpenTo.

Innovation Delivery: Quality is God

Tijn van Elderen

Quality is God—or, at least, that's what I took from Robert Pirsig's book *Zen and the Art of Motorcycle Maintenance.*

In this book, the author takes the reader on a journey of an internal battle with himself and a struggling relationship with his son, all the while trying to figure out what Quality really is. He finally bridges the gap between objective and subjective quality by calling the bridge God. Therefore, Quality equals God.

I recognize this struggle to define a particular concept when I try to define what the success of innovation realization is. For me Innovation Delivery (ID) is two sides of the same coin—the coin of subjective and objective Quality. The objective side depends on the measurable part of ID, such as the structure of the process, the (f)actual list of requirements, and the performance of the end result against this list of requirements, etc. The subjective side depends on how consumers perceive the end result and its performance against the (often more fuzzy) core proposition of a product or service—is it good looking enough, does it have the required appeal, etc., for the price?

Now anyone experienced in the innovation process will tell you that certain steps in the process have to be followed: jump through the hoops, dot those I's and cross those T's. But do we really take the time to consciously and meticulously go through this process?

I think in reality we find ourselves juggling with time, money and specifications. For the sake of time to market, budget reductions, and such, we cut corners and jump to conclusions before defining the real need or problem, and often simulate testing rather than do real testing (for example, we once had a supplier test a cheese slicer on a bar of soap, since he didn't have cheese available!).

In order to be better, faster and cheaper than the competition, we seem to only focus on the latter two. While I realize that budgets aren't endless and time waits for no one, often it's being BETTER that makes us stand out and brings success—especially if you want to be the best (not the cheapest or the fastest). Like playing golf, or doing the perfect breaststroke, it takes 10,000 hours of practice before you do it right.

I firmly believe that ID depends on the Quality of Delivery. If you *do* dot the I's and cross the T's, you increase the potential of the objective quality. Then, you need to work hard on creativity. Once you've done this, you can only pray that God appears to build the bridge.

Tijn van Elderen, Brabantia, www.brabantia.com

Exploring New Segments
Via Cross-Sectored Cooperation

Patrick Essers

How do you increase innovation when budgets are being cut? How do you create verticals that will bring new connections alive? How do you deliver faster than the market expects? And how do you address customer needs in a different segment?

The state of large co-operative innovation is evolving. An early stage of customer involvement with the close co-operation of powerful partners has become the credo of our initiative.

A collaboration setup like our Seedlinqs initiative ensures pooling knowledge so as to develop new multi-media business segments. Until recently you only watched TV on your television, used the Internet strictly on your computer and sent text messages by phone. Today, this is all integrated. Networks are increasingly merging, and our expertise lies in amalgamating all these different technologies. However, developing such applications requires understanding consumer needs, which in some verticals is unexplored. As we realized the importance of our network and applications matching up, our interest in the matter was aroused.

Public partners believe that only multinational companies can create such an environment and generate the necessary momentum to speed things up. Look at Philips and their High Tech Campus. They believe that you need an ecosystem of companies that collectively use their expertise to create products and solutions with a competitive advantage. Such cooperation in a cluster of large and small/medium-sized enterprises is very attractive and effective.

A second major reason for cooperation is that different national markets are unique. While networks and infrastructures may be similar everywhere, how multimedia products are put on the market differs from place to place. It is smarter to use specific regional knowledge rather than assume that only large organizations are good at developing new products. Innovations often emerge from small businesses and the initiatives of smart individuals, and there's little reason for them to see value in sharing their ideas with a big corporation. Yet many smart innovation paths end when they actually need to be scaled, and there is insufficient capacity to provide quality service or produce larger numbers. Seedlinqs gives small businesses access to a massive network in a very approachable way, making it easier for a great product to hit the market.

Besides contributions from the founding partners, Seedlinqs has also acquired financial incentives from government and industry. This contributes to the three main goals of Seedlinqs: autonomy, dynamism and self-support. Seedlinqs should have the right and the power of self-government, a continuous and productive change in innovation lines, and be able to meet its needs by its own efforts or project output. In order to achieve these goals, a number of very specific choices have had to be made. Therefore, Seedlinqs is also working on funding for accelerating innovation and development projects. Grants for risky development projects, but also favorable loans and venture capital products to the market or to scale development are germane to this phase of the project. That means companies, research institutions, education and government can all work closely together. Collaboration between private and public domains result in new, innovative services and solutions—whether it's a solution on therapy compliance for cardiology patients, or a connected car service where riders can access network and cloud-based applications, or a broadcasted video message introducing a new movie.

In the multimedia wilderness, we opted to focus our innovation lines on three areas. We've only seen the beginning of the massive data growth driven by smart phones and other mobile devices. New business models will emerge with so-called "co-opetition" among operators, where they share platforms and build scale together around applications. There are fresh markets to address, and companies like Ericsson must consider developing for customers beyond traditional telecom operators such as cable and television companies—education, governments, healthcare, transport and utility companies, for example. There's a huge need in these industries for telecommunication services, and Seedlinqs is taking notice. Mergers and acquisitions are good for buying a certain market, but they kill creativity in every co-development; we're always looking elsewhere instead of creating our own supply chain.

Patrick Essers of Ericsson has a successful track record in New Business Development and Innovations. www.ericsson.com

Delivering Innovation Is Speaking the Same Language

Dries Faems

The majority of manufacturing companies seem to realize that innovation is fundamental to long-term company success based on a survey of manufacturing firms we recently conducted in the Netherlands. This is proven by the fact that, when questioned, the majority of companies admitted that they decided not to cut research and development during times of economic crisis. Yet there are clearly a number of challenges and bottlenecks.

The first important finding from our research is that few companies speak a common internal language when it comes to innovation. Many manufacturing companies talk in fairly general terms about innovation, with the term being broadly used to refer to everything that is "new" in some form or other. It's important to realize, however, that innovation doesn't just refer to improving existing products and markets (incremental innovation), but also to creating new products and services (radical innovation). What's more, successfully realizing the different forms of innovation frequently requires different activities (exploitive versus explorative), different sorts of people (analytical versus intuitive), and different management styles (mechanistic versus organic).

Most manufacturing companies consider both the exploitation and the exploration of existing products and markets important, yet when we take a good look at the actual investment behavior of these companies a healthy balance of exploitation and exploration isn't always evident. Smaller companies tend to invest mainly in exploration, while large companies invest in exploitation. This suggests a need for better strategic alignment of what is said to be important (the innovation goals), and what actually happens (the innovation investments).

To improve the strategic alignment of innovation goals and investments, companies need to systematically evaluate and formalize the two aspects. And yet, many companies are still far from mapping out and following up on their innovation projects and performance. We would advise companies to define a limited number of innovation performance indicators, and then meticulously follow and evaluate them.

Innovation only adds value for a company if the entire company supports it. This means a culture must develop where employees from different departments and different levels are encouraged to think about and contribute to innovation.

Contrary to many management gurus, we don't believe that the management team can force such a culture. But it can facilitate innovation culture by actively investing in the innovation efforts of its workforce. We're also convinced that more possibilities exist in many companies for additional investment in personnel practices that stimulate innovation, such as paying attention to creativity when recruiting new personnel, evaluating the creativity of current employees and providing financial rewards for innovative behavior.

The challenge of finishing innovation projects on time and within budget appears to be one of the bottlenecks companies face; in many companies, management were seen as weak when it came to innovation processes. In addition, there are many human resource practices that manufacturing companies can use to actually encourage innovation and creativity in their employees.

In short, our points for innovation are:

- Develop a common internal innovation language that will enable discussions to take place on the importance, the complexity and the various forms of innovation

- Develop performance indicators that enable innovation projects to be monitored and evaluated. In this way, the company can learn more about both completed innovation projects and ones in progress

- Give employees opportunity and space to develop innovative activities. Support these activities by implementing selection, training and remuneration programs that explicitly underline the importance of innovation. This will in turn create a broad, innovation culture throughout the company.

- Invest in partnerships with external partners—customers, suppliers, knowledge institutes and the competition. Try not to limit these partnerships to a local level, but also look abroad.

Dries Faems is a Full Professor of Innovation & Organization at the University of Groningen, and an Affiliated Researcher at the Katholieke Universiteit Leuven. Professor Faems' current research focuses on the performance implications of alliance portfolios.

Innovation Spaces:
How to Foster the Delivery
of Innovation

Anne-Laure Fayard

Companies want informal interaction because of the collaboration and new idea generation associated with it. They design their offices with this in mind, but new idea generation, or invention, is only half the story. The second half consists of innovating—implementing ideas and applying them in the marketplace—which is equally important. If office space can foster new idea generation, how can it also foster innovation? Neither innovation nor invention take place in a vacuum; spaces matter in supporting prototyping and cross-collaboration, two essential practices for successful innovation.

Spaces to prototype...
Innovation results from a lot of inventions and a lot of failures. To know whether something is going to work, you need to try it out, and test it as early as possible. Prototyping, or experimenting and playing with ideas, is at the core of the practices of design and innovation consultancies such as IDEO, Engine and Live|Work. Visiting the London IDEO office for the first time, I was welcomed by the cardboard prototype of a car sitting in the middle of the entrance. What a great reminder to both IDEO associates and visitors like me that trying things out was "okay." Being able to leave a prototype in the middle of the office for all to see not only allows the team to go back and work on it whenever they want, but invites others to give feedback. And prototypes (even unsuccessful ones) might inspire another team.

Prototyping isn't about just claiming it as a value, or posting a list of brain-storming rules on your walls. You have to provide space and time for people to prototype. Proximity also matters if you want others to comment upon, and be inspired by, the proposed ideas. Private meeting rooms (sometimes with windows or glass walls) where people can freely explore crazy ideas are useful, especially in companies where the culture isn't supportive of crazy ideas. Of course, support for prototyping doesn't always mean having a cardboard car in the hallway or walls covered with maps, pictures, and Post-It notes like at Engine; it can be something as simple as allowing people to have messy desks, or to occupy a meeting room for several days without having to clean it.

...And cross-collaborate

From idea generation to marketplace, innovation involves every function in an organization—from R&D to consumer research, marketing and sales. A marketing vice president at a large multinational firm insists that successful cross-team collaboration requires a sense of proximity and what she calls "a space for expression." Even when teams are distributed across functions and geographies, supporting encounters through spaces (including official meetings, team building or creativity sessions and informal dinners) is crucial. New social network tools like Yammer or Ideajam that connect and share ideas within organizations can also be used to build a collaborative space.

As the increased distribution of work blurs boundaries within a company, and as both virtual teams and experiments with open innovation proliferate, space matters more than ever. Think of the development of co-working spaces in various cities around the world where a platform for idea flow exists, creating a community of people who have different jobs but want to share ideas. Communities such as OpenIDEO (openideo.com) are a great example of social innovation. A few visits to the site show how it provides proximity with an incredible group of creative and enthusiastic thinkers while allowing relative privacy in the comments thread. Permission is at the heart of OpenIDEO; the tone set in the challenge brief and the comments of the community managers establishes that spirit of freedom.

To design spaces that support innovation, you should aim to balance the "3 Ps":

- Proximity: Do people have reasons to come and stay in a space?

- Privacy: Can they control access, i.e., minimize interruptions or eavesdropping?

- Permission: What are the cultural norms and social conventions around communication and working?

Anne-Laure Fayard is Assistant Professor of Management at the Polytechnic Institute of New York University. www.bazartropicando.com/alfwebsite/index.html

Curating Innovation and Entrepreneurship

Auke Ferwerda

In the Netherlands, talent is plentiful but entrepreneurship is lacking. The triple helix of innovation doesn't function at its best, so talent fails to reach the market and knowledge is lost. The secret of innovation hubs like Silicon Valley and Bangalore is the power of cooperation from many organizations with an interest in developing new products or services. In the Netherlands, we need to follow this example and bring industry, knowledge institutions and government together in moving towards an integrated innovation policy. The formation of the Media Guild is one such attempt, an organization establishing partnerships and collaborations to promote innovation strategies that create opportunities for startups in the creative sector.

Meeting Place

Traditional incubation doesn't lead to results in the Dutch marketplace; the focus needs to be on coaching and guiding talent towards a successful business future. Media Guild provides a network that connects young entrepreneurs with leading companies and investors. The aim is to have a short, valuable incubation process that leads to a stable, well-connected organization. Ambitious initiatives in the creative industry get the opportunity to develop their innovative and technological ideas in a networked environment. Media Guild is essentially a meeting place and a platform where knowledge institutes, large corporations and small businesses can connect with schools, universities and creatives. Long-term relationships within the helix lead to successful incubation.

Dutch Valley

In the Dutch Valley network, Media Guild is developing the leading national incubation and acceleration platform, where the mission is to curate innovation and entrepreneurship. The Netherlands still lacks a truly entrepreneurial culture, but Media Guild is working with universities and businesses in Dutch Valley to make entrepreneurship more attractive. It does this through business plan competitions and collaboration with the global entrepreneur network Startup Weekend.

Dutch Valley focuses on obtaining and sharing knowledge, which stimulates entrepreneurship and new collaborations between incubators and investors. The main goal is connecting with international innovation clusters. Dutch Valley takes the lead in the creation of European Valley—enhancing European cooperation in the innovation chain.

Auke Ferwerda, *Waag Society*

The Venture Challenge

Hans Le Fever

The name of this regular business plan competition in the Life Sciences field also illustrates the issues that surround bringing academic research findings to commercial fruition. It all starts with scientists discovering patentable findings in the course of their research. With the establishment of technology transfer offices at all universities, applying for a patent is common practice. However, this is only the first step towards getting full value from findings that could lead to cutting-edge drugs, diagnostic tests, agronomic analysis tools or bio-based chemical processes.

At this junction, some scientists decide to embark on a new topic of research; others require more than a publication and a patent on the shelf for their efforts. They are intrigued by what's needed to get their finding actually used outside the lab. They embark upon a difficult but rewarding journey, sometimes through the Venture Challenge mentioned above. In this type of business plan, competition scientists and more business-oriented people are challenged to explore where the true value of their finding lies ("Who is the customer?") and what the best route to reaching that goal is.

A crucial mental shift for a scientist is comprehension of the customer's point of view. Usually scientists can tell you in their sleep how fantastic their technology is, but are often less verbose on what precise problem their technology solves. The whole process of determining customer need, how best to fill that need and what value a customer would place on a solution is best done in an off-site, safe environment (because there's a substantial difference between academic speak and business lingo, so a great deal of patience is needed for mutual understanding).

There's also a difference in thinking patterns; scientists think deductively, while business developers tend to be more practical. There's also much to be learnt about what could be called being "economical with the truth", leaving out any and all defensive terminology that scientists use against possible attacks on the scientific validity of their statements.

When a scientist understands the tricks of a business perspective, it becomes like any other challenge: they are proud to have mastered something new, energized by new perspectives and keen to move further towards commercialization. Fellow business coach Math Kohnen and I run a Venture Challenge for NGI (Netherlands Genomics Initiative) through eNovITe; being scientists turned businessmen themselves, we're only too keen to help others on that rewarding path.

Hans Le Fever is a business coach at eNovITe. www.venturechallenge.nl, www.enovite.com

The Entrepreneur as Driver of the Knowledge Triangle

Alexander von Gabain

Many Europeans believe that top-class research and education will *always* result in innovation. But a closer look at how research and education creates innovative chains of added value within the U.S. (and more recently within the emerging markets) reveals that the entrepreneur plays a crucial role within the "knowledge triangle" of business, education and research. He or she can unlock the knowledge and education found within R&D institutions to drive potentials into new business creation.

Innovative entrepreneurship is a rare species in Europe since teachers, students and graduates of European universities seldom see opportunities to translate their knowledge and education into innovative products and services. This negative trend is facilitated by:

- Prevailing averse public opinion towards entrepreneurship, ownership and risk-taking

- No visible and outstanding entrepreneurial role models that compare with Americans like Gates (Microsoft), Zuckerberg (Facebook) and Boyer (Genentech)

- Unsupportive attitudes by academia towards colleagues and trainees who seek entrepreneurial chances instead of pursuing a career in academia

- A lack of incentive structures and risk capital, ironically counteracted by an excess of red tape thwarting innovative business setups

To overcome this innovation gap, an independent body of the European Union called the EIT (European Institute of Innovation and Technology) was set up three years ago to implement Knowledge and Innovation Communities (KICs). KICs integrate public and private research organizations, innovative industries, higher education institutions, investors and spin-offs as legal entities.

The first three KICs assemble five or six European hotspots of excellence with a strong reputation for research and education to focus on specific societal challenges such as renewable energy. The EIT acts as a high-impact innovation fund by providing seed money to the KICs, led and run by a CEO on the basis of their respective business plans. This ensures that the innovation power of the integrated hotspots is optimally utilized to create innovative business and services within the thematic fields of each KIC.

Students, trainees and professional experts working within a KIC are educated through degree programs and entrepreneurship courses that award an EIT label. The EIT supports and fosters the KICs towards innovative entrepreneurship; the first three KICs have already been successful in forming 16 hotspots across Europe. The EIT and the KICs are designed to continuously learn from each other; based on feedback from the first round of KICs, the EIT is aiming for a second round of investment from 2014 onwards.

Alexander von Gabain is Chairman Elect of the EIT Governing Board. http://eit.europa.eu

Challenge Management

Han Gerrits, Rogier van Kralingen

The work field of innovation is rapidly changing. The rise of the 24/7 society means we're faced with increasingly faster changes in technological, political, consumer and business developments, forcing us to react ever faster. And the rise of the network society transforms the ways we share knowledge and create. Apart from traditional brainstorming, we can now contact creative partners all over the world, have online competitions and use the Web to dramatically increase the speed of knowledge sharing. Anyone not connected to this transformation will be unable to successfully innovate in this day and age. We firmly believe this because, as a software company, we've had front row seats during the network society developments.

For instance, take the many faces of crowdsourcing. The approach a company chooses for crowdsourcing has everything to do with the eventual outcome. For simple challenges, the general public can get involved in generating ideas. By working together with the consumer, we can increase the chances of successful innovation. For more specific challenges (finding a new logo, for instance) specialized crowds are available on the web.

Once these challenges become more complex, many organizations get caught in a catch-22; they need to innovate quickly and have the knowledge to do it, but lack the ability to connect with an appropriate knowledge base. An intranet usually gets built as a rule, but most intranets aren't dedicated idea management tools. Quality, quantity and speed of innovation can suffer severely.

Then an even bigger problem occurs: if you connect hundreds or even thousands of people to a network, that network needs to be monitored and kept in check. People have to be inspired and stimulated to take part in the challenges. Just because a network exists doesn't automatically mean it'll be run successfully.

The most common mistake we have seen over the years is companies using their standard intranet facilities to start large-scale Idea Generation. These aren't dedicated Idea Management Tools, nor are they run by professionals who know how to stimulate people to take part. A technician is not the same as a community or challenge manager. More than half our clients have lost months, or even years, in innovation time by initiating challenges that have, in the end, demotivated personnel because they couldn't get it running successfully. Nowadays, losing time to unsuccessful (external or internal) crowdsourcing can be costly indeed, and can cause you to lose your competitive edge.

Something we call "The solution Challenge Management," can be described as the psychological and sociological field of challenging people to come up and enhance great ideas. We've seen magical things happen when large groups of people are connected in the right way.

Since embarking on its first challenge, one telecom company saved tens of millions of dollars. More than a thousand new product ideas appeared to another fast mover. An employment agency has seen a vast treasure of accumulated worldwide and decade-long knowledge rise to the surface. And all this always—amazingly—happens in just two to six weeks.

Besides generating ideas for innovation, challenges can also be utilized in the product development process. We see organizations using challenges to gather knowledge and expertise needed to develop ideas into products. Even more, some organizations are using the crowd of consumers to reflect on first versions of products to ensure that the product really fits the needs of targeted users. In general, innovation processes are opening up for outsiders and we think challenges are a good way to guarantee that outside participation delivers value.

Idea Management Software and Challenge Management will fast become the new paradigms in innovation, and these developments will greatly benefit the outcome of innovation in today's networked society. By doing this, any company can become an Innovation Factory.

Han Gerrits is a Professor at VU University Amsterdam and Founder/CEO of Innovation Factory.
Rogier van Kralingen is a young and upcoming innovation author. www.innovationfactory.eu

A Brief Take on
Day-to-Day Innovation

Giancarlo Ghiretti

Innovation has many faces. It can be revolutionary, creating new products and industries and potentially changing the lives of millions of people. Or it can just consist of small improvements that generate added value for customers on specific topics, define the details of a company and its processes, or become crucial to the execution of a business plan. We call these innovations the "small innovations." They aren't celebrated in magazines or television shows, nor do they create instant millionaires in IPOs. But without those small day-to-day innovations, it's doubtful whether the revolutionary ideas we all admire would ever become successful businesses.

How does an entrepreneur take ideas and turn them into processes, and then into products (or services)? Every entrepreneur faces a series of questions on a daily basis, including how to turn their idea into a success, how to create a company, and how the manufacturing process should be developed. There are further questions regarding the logistical process, the marketing plan, invoices, logos, designs, colors, literature, communications, and PR. It's mindboggling! And every single one of these questions is crucial to the success of the idea.

The entrepreneur has to make countless decisions that will affect the ultimate success of the larger idea. Many of these decisions will result in small innovations. Taking ideas, processes, plans, management tips, etc., and adapting them to the specifics of each individual company comprises the heart and soul of our daily work as entrepreneurs. All these small innovations will eventually lead to the execution and success of a larger innovative idea.

I strongly believe that communication is key for this process to happen. In our specific case we run an open office where each member of our team is always encouraged to speak his or her mind. We believe in allowing for difference of opinion around a specific topic. For this process to work, there can be no such thing as wrong answers or ideas. All feedback is received in a kind of round table that often leads to conclusions, decisions and yet more unanswered questions. It's a constructive process that leads to improvement and small innovations.

By continuously running through this process at different levels of the company, and around different topics and questions, it's possible to increase workforce motivation, loyalty and productivity while fostering communication and small innovation. Our idea-bouncing process leads to better decision-making and innovation, creating added value for our customers and stakeholders.

I invite you to use this strategy during your next lunch with a colleague. Tell him or her about an idea or topic that is on your mind and ask for an opinion. And see what happens. I believe the result of the conversation will surprise you in a positive way. And hopefully a small (or large) innovation will happen.

Giancarlo Ghiretti, *Virmax Limited*

A Successful Innovation Team Can Innovate in Any Industry

Iwan Göbel

The power of innovation is deeply underestimated, particularly in times of crisis. That's exactly when a company needs a competitive edge in order to survive a shrinking market and cope with consumers who are making more conscientious choices. In such times, price and innovation are deciding factors.

For years, a small team of specialists at Burton Car Company have been developing an average of one product a week, assisted further by a peloton of small, specialized companies. The products they work on are diverse: a sports car, urinals, garden tables, chairs, a book on sustainable renovation, car parts, and a vibrator for an electric toothbrush. A successful innovation team can innovate in practically any industry; this tactic earned us the title of best entrepreneurs in the Netherlands.

Our understanding of innovation is simple:

- Success starts with a good idea and a small enthusiastic team of decision makers. If you try to make soup with 100 cooks, you'll get a mediocre, flavorless soup. Use three or four cooks and you'll get a delicious soup—though perhaps not to everyone's taste.

- Take negative people off the team and encourage critique, courage, reality and persistence.

- Develop a good marketing plan. Most new products get stranded in the final stage because of bad marketing, so the marketing plan should be brief and clear. Involve the marketing person right from the initial spark of the idea, product or service.

- Choose a sustainable product. Sustainability is a necessity, not a trend.

- Build around customer satisfaction, not the product.

- Consider subsidies that may be available and help with development, but understand that they consume time.

- Aim for the long term, not a quick success, and consider working with another company that can add value through its name, distribution, know-how, innovation or capital.

Iwan Göbel is CEO at Burton Car Company BV and a speaker at the Speakers Academy on sustainable entrepreneurship.

Delivery of Innovation with Boxed Refining: Technology Option in Search of Business Cases

Hans Gosselink, Arian Nijmeijer and Alfred Mutsaars

In 1998, a team of large-scale processing researchers working for large refineries was inspired by a concept that went against the grain. Despite working in an area where economies of scale are important, the team took on a concept of boxed refineries, a flexible system of small-scale processing in sea-containers that could be used to upgrade biomass. Their challenge was to then compete with economies of scale by applying economies of numbers—in this case large numbers of small, identical, and mass-produced boxes. The concept was funded for many years from corporate strategic innovation and gamechanger budgets.

From a technology perspective, the first step was designing boxed refineries based on physical processes such as blending and membrane separation and making use of externally and internally available technology. They then had to find business cases for the concept in order to balance the technology push with market pull. The research team started talking with business developers, and came up with two totally different options in the first wave:

- A boxed fuel upgrader to enhance gasoline at commercial fuel depots

- A waterbox to enable water purification in rural areas

Boxed fuel upgraders were technically successful in pilots at two European Shell fuel depots in the period 2003-2006, but the business case and strategic fit weren't strong enough to lead to commercial implementation. The waterbox was successfully demonstrated in 2003 by implementation of a 1 m³/hr clean drinking water unit at a Shell retail station in the Karoo Desert in South Africa. It provided the best drinking water in the region. Another success followed in 2005 when an NGO in Morocco purchased a waterbox to provide the Ait Chaib village with clean and safe drinking water.

The waterbox connected the team with representatives of the former Shell Solar Southern Africa (SSSA), who had the Ngceleni Coastal District under investigation and project deployment for 5 years. The area had the poorest municipality in South Africa, with 76% unemployment. The SSSA team built a mini-grid based on solar and wind power in 2003 to provide local villages with electricity. However, the local people needed economic activity to purchase the electricity. In a series of area workshops where Shell employees with various specialties had numerous discussions with local community members and authorities, a new concept was born, designed and gained support. The concept involved enhanced agriculture on unused farmland for food production as well as biomass for bio-oil via boxed biomass processing units. Selling the bio-oil for biofuels production would provide the community with the required economic activity. However, final business case for Shell wasn't strong enough in an internal competition for investment budgets and the complete concept was handed to a local entrepreneur.

Although the above applications (boxed fuel upgrader, boxed biomass processing and waterbox) didn't result in a commercial take-off, it developed the research team's technical and implementation skills, credibility and internal company network. As a result, new applications closer to the core of Shell's operations were successfully identified.

The case of boxed refining is a clear example of a very ambitious and dedicated research team generating new technology options, and their search for the right business cases/partners to enable real innovation delivery.

__Hans Gosselink__ is Regional Manager of Innovation Biodomain for Shell Projects & Technology, Amsterdam. He co-authored this article with __Arian Nijmeijer__ and __Alfred Mutsaars__. www.shell.com

Delivering Old Bread
to a New Market

Rob de Graaf

If any phase of the innovation process deserves extra attention, it's the Delivery phase. Research illustrates that this phase drives the success of a new product in the market. No matter how well the Discovery and Development phases have been dealt with, if you aren't doing your Innovation Delivery right, all has been in vain. Therefore, the Delivery phase should be a major part of the innovation budget. Only after a successful launch of the innovation can it be handed over to the marketing & sales function.

The interesting thing about an innovation process is that it's nested—the Discovery and Development phases also have Delivery processes. Launching an idea to get it funded for Development, and releasing all relevant documentation for Delivery, can be seen as Delivery stages for these phases. So the innovation team has experience doing it, even if they don't realize it. At the same time, the Delivery phase itself also has a Discovery and a Development stage.

This can be illustrated by a case from the Dutch Bakery sector. In an effort facilitated by the Innovation Leadership Network, participants from across the sector came up with solutions for more than 80 million loaves of excess bread per year. As consumers demand fresh bread until closing time, bakers are stuck with bread that's left over when the store closes - a terrible waste of a key fiber source in our diet.

In the Discovery phase, one of the teams came up with the concept of upcycling bread, i.e. cutting, marinating, and drying it in a cooling oven. This creates a nutritious snack, somewhat similar to potato chips. This is a completely new market for most bakeries and was well received at the concept presentation to the whole bakery sector, with a ready-to-eat prototype available only 60 days after the start of the process. You could argue it was a great delivery of the end of the Discovery phase.

Next, the Development phase started to get good recipes and marinades, nutritional facts, information on processing, pricing, etc. After about 6 months, all the ingredients for an industrialized upcycled bread snack were ready for the whole bakery sector to add to its portfolio. Once more, Delivery was successful; both industrial and traditional bakeries were very willing to take it up. Actually, some conflicts arose as to who could get the stuff first!

Then the Innovation Delivery phase started. It turned out that not every bakery was able to convert the two prior successes into a successful launch of the product. As the product was new, consumers were hesitant to buy it, as they did not know what it was. Only when the concept was explained and people could actually try the product, did consumers show interest. Those bakeries that gave special attention to the newness of the product, the values it held for their customers, and the attributes of the product delivering those values, succeeded in convincing their customer base that upcycled bread was an excellent alternative for other snacks, like potato chips.

With active in-store promotion, trained staff, and a good story, consumers started to acquire the taste for the new product after a few months, and came back for more! Simply adding the product to the portfolio did not lead to adoption of the new product. Interestingly, the upcycled bread now sells at more than 100 times the price of the old bread that became pig food. In fact, this old bread product sells at about five times the price of fresh bread!

The case shows how innovation at the Delivery phase is essential for success. All bakers had the same starting point after Development and the same ingredients available, but only those who paid sufficient attention to the Innovation Delivery phase itself were successful.

Rob de Graaf is Director of the Innovation Leadership Network. www.innovationleadership.eu

Alliances as Innovation Delivery Accelerator

Alfred Griffioen

Having the right plan or a bright idea is the first step; step two is the execution. In some cases, new insights can be incorporated directly in your market approach, production technology or cost structure to achieve immediate competitive advantage. However, this process is often slowed down by the lack of new resources or competencies. If all innovations were in line with your current business, life would be a lot easier.

Alliances are an important means of obtaining the right resources and competences at low costs and low risk. The alternative in most cases is to hire new staff, train existing personnel or to do research and development yourself. This requires considerable time and effort and may lead to a loss of momentum. Hiring consultants or contracting a supplier is another alternative; although this leads to quicker results, you won't be the exclusive owner of the solution.

An alliance is an agreement between two or more independent parties that is entered into in order to advance common goals and secure common interests. Risk sharing is an important characteristic of an alliance, which distinguishes collaboration from a transactional relationship. In an alliance, outcomes like market penetration, technological development or costs are uncertain at the outset; both parties can either benefit or suffer accordingly.

The search for an alliance partner should always start with an assessment of what resources or competences are needed, and what the profile of the perfect partner would be. Prospective partners that have a similar size and organizational culture, with nearby headquarters, and previous experience with other collaborations offer the best chance of a long-lasting relationship.

The good news is that alliances can be structured deliberately, and aspects can be modeled and even standardized. Through our research we've identified ten types of alliances, including franchising, co-branding and shared investments. For each type, it is possible to list the most important variables for splitting revenues and costs, and to find best practices for assigning decision power, risks and intellectual property rights. This way, the relatively unknown skill of structuring and managing alliances can be learned easily.

The types used most frequently in the case of technological innovations are joint R&D and technology licensing, which form opposite ends of a spectrum. In the case of technology licensing, the technology in question is already defined and only its value needs to be split. In the case of joint R&D, what really matters is the collaboration between researchers, so that the alliance offers a framework in which knowledge is freely shared and developments can be steered effectively.

In our daily practice we find many companies simply start a collaboration with the first partner that happens to come along, leaving the joint business model and deal structure to be developed along the way. This can be a perfect learning experience, but isn't the way to enhance the likelihood of success. Alliance management is a competence that should be embedded in the organization. An extra PowerPoint slide about alliances in the strategy presentation, a structured selection process for partners, and a set of special KPIs for managing an alliance are examples of means to improve both your alliance and innovation execution skills.

Alfred Griffioen assists companies in creating and optimizing strategic collaboration. www.alliance-experts.com

Simplification:
A Shortcut to Innovation Delivery

Theo Groen

Exactly one century ago, the famous economist Joseph Schumpeter explained in his book *Theorie der wirtschaftlichen Entwicklung* the different mentalities of innovators and entrepreneurs. To paraphrase a long text in German: The inventor comes with new ideas and the entrepreneur brings them to the market. Unfortunately, in many technology-driven companies both minds live in the same brain.

How do you recognize a technology-driven company? The innovator-entrepreneur has a technological background. The company has a research and development department filled with engineers and scientists. Often the company's main technology is reflected in its name. The company's communication highlights technical aspects of the products, showing shiny devices and copious technical specifications.

In such an environment, there's strong cultural and professional pressure to put technology before the needs of clients and to make more and more sophisticated products. This prolongs and complicates the innovation process. It can result in oversized products with a range of functions that go beyond the needs of individual customers. It increases the risk of both severe defects in new products and customer disappointment. Altogether, that cultural pressure results in higher R&D costs, delayed market introduction, loss of market share, and a time delay before the new product generates sufficient cash flow.

Can putting more efforts in R&D solve the problem? No, because this perpetuates the technology push. This situation requires a different approach; the company must learn to think "against the grain". A powerful method is to simplify products (both existing and in development), suppressing the disposition to add new technology. Such innovations use only proven technology and are made from materials, devices and parts the company already has available. This method has major advantages:

- It opens windows to new product market combinations. Smaller-sized customers prefer simplified and cheaper products for private and mobile users. Lightweight and frugal variants are attractive because they are more sustainable (energy consumption, use of raw materials) or have lower operational costs (medical devices).

- Simpler products generally take less time to hit the market, with favorable effects on costs and profitability. Innovation process risks are reduced because these products are less complex and built from components the company has experience with.

- It creates a new source of creativity, forcing the company to look at its innovation portfolio in a different way—not only as (new) products and technological specifications, but also at the level of existing product components, with all kinds of possibilities to form new combinations between them.

- It's hard for many customers to participate in the design of a brand-new, complex product. They find it easier to join in R&D and marketing meetings to discuss (simplified) variants of existing products. Customer participation can yield valuable information for the innovation process—especially about what value the new product has in the daily practice of the customer's organization.

Theo Groen is co-owner of Prisma & Partners, with over 20 years experience as an innovation process consultant. www.prismaenpartners.nl

The Internal Innovation Implementation Phase

André Groeneveld

Successful innovations are made up of two steps: having a good idea and successful market implementation. It's generally understood that there needs to be a good idea, and all kinds of initiatives are taken in order to produce good ideas. Also, the benefit of successful market implementation is obvious to everyone and massive amounts of time and effort are spent on it. This seems obvious and simple—but it isn't.

This simple model lacks a third step between the other two, which can be referred to as internal business implementation. It is crucial to the innovation process.

Innovative ideas can be collected in professional brainstorm sessions, where considerable attention is given to the organization's buy-in. Representatives of other departments and/or decision makers are often invited to these sessions. This should naturally create a good level of internal business implementation, but seldom does. Brainstorm session ideas are carefully worked out, possibly supported by market research, then selected for introduction; it is at this point that things often go wrong.

You see, now the rest of the organization is put to work. The product or service actually has to be made, which means introducing it into the company's systems, pilot productions, planning, and so forth. Suddenly, there's no space for these plans anymore. Small orders of necessary components are hard to come by. There's a sense of wanting to deliver the standard products or services first, and that the newfangled ideas get short shrift. The result is delay, postponement—even abandonment.

In the end, it has to be the organization itself that forms one of the critical steps towards successful innovation. In order to achieve better innovations faster, more attention to the company itself must be paid. Adding an extra step in the innovation process can do this: the internal innovation implementation phase.

André Groeneveld, FrieslandCampina Domo

The Crucial Human Factor in Innovation

Georges Haou

The quality of innovation process output in firms is a direct function of the talent and motivation of the staff carrying them out. Management and business schools tend to exaggerate the importance of tools and theories in effective innovation delivery, when actually it comes down to the human factor. Management must *make more time* to deal with the critical aspects of motivating staff, while developing both innovative spirit and entrepreneurial energy. This is the motto of my recent book *Resolving the Innovation Paradox* (www.innovationparadox.com).

Integrating new hires

Laura, unit manager in the research organization MatLab, always organizes a party soon after a new hire joins her unit. This workplace get-together provides an opportunity to introduce the new hire to the community. It also sends a positive message of welcome, celebrating the new arrival and strengthening the team. Laura feels that parties should be held when people join the company, rather than when they leave. She also shares her office with new hires for their first three months on the job. In this way, Laura is readily available for questions and can gradually inform the new hires and introduce them to people coming to her office.

The manager as coach

First-line managers must carve out time to act as a resource when needed, be discreet when the professionals need to concentrate on a crucial piece of work, and engage in dialogue when the person is ready to receive input.

In our turbulent business environment, managers are so busy with operational tasks that they have difficulty finding time to nurture trusting and inspiring relationships with their staff. "Being busy" is a lame excuse for allowing urgent situations to take precedence over important ones.

Developing an entrepreneurial perspective and the technical professional's business sense must be a top priority of managers who practice "management by walking around". This begins with hiring; managers should consciously hire staff better than themselves, but how many actually do? The firm must attract candidates with an entrepreneurial profile, which entails a lack of bureaucracy. Who makes Silicon Valley, California, and Cambridge, UK successful? Researchers-entrepreneurs.

Developing project leaders in an entrepreneurial perspective

The insufficient number of high-performance project managers is a major bottleneck in technology companies. The problem is compounded by the fact that the innovation process is increasingly carried out in complex, multi-actor projects, "federating" a lot of inputs external to the firm.

The richness of team diversity

Our increasingly interdependent world is thankfully not homogeneous. The richness of its diversity must be managed as a highly positive asset. A powerful way to do this is for managers to master several languages, including the 'useless', 'dead' languages of Latin and Greek. This opens and trains the mind in unique ways. Knowing a non-native language goes well beyond conversing in it; it provides considerable enrichment, allowing a vision of the world from a different point of view.

Partly due to its cosmopolitan perspective, Europe is the world's best-equipped region for brilliant success in the 21st Century. For effectively leveraging these assets, however, both better leadership and more courage are needed.

Georges Haou is Professor at IMD, Switzerland, and acts as adviser to companies on the management of R&D innovation, entrepreneurship and technology commercialization.

Innovation in Россия, Alternative Financing for Innovation

Harry Harbers

On a bitterly cold wintery day in Moscow, I received a call from a friend who worked locally in banking and had just announced his resignation. After congratulating him, I asked which bank he was moving to. He explained that he wanted to start a new self-storage company in Moscow. An old friend from school was the CEO and owner of LagerBox, the third largest German self-storage operator, and they both saw a great opportunity in Russia. I silently asked myself why anyone would make such a brave move in a country known to be difficult for startups given red tape and so forth. My curiosity piqued, I offered to look over the business plan and company structure.

Having worked within the Russian market for over 15 years, I know first-hand how hard it is to make relatively straightforward processes happen in Russia. There's a solution for every problem; it just takes longer, with more effort and usually more creativity. As an example, the set up of an OOO (Russian LLC) normally takes a few months, including various trips to the notary and tax office. Just waiting in line at the tax office can take up to 6 hours—again, I speak from experience!

Upon reading the business plan, I found the possibilities for opportunity intriguing. Moscow has around 15 million inhabitants; in mid-2010 there were only 4 self-storage sites, all of which had opened in the previous 18 months. London has the same number of people, yet there are over 350 self-storage sites! If anything, demand should be higher in the Russian market, with its tiny apartments and climate-driven seasonal storage requirements. Clearly the Russian market was "ready" for self-storage service.To make a long story short, I joined the effort and began setting up the legal and fiscal structures, (re-)writing the business plan, drafting the required documentation and most importantly, fundraising. To give the company a proper start, we had to raise 6 million Euro to secure funding for three initial locations.

We discussed at length on how to source 6 million Euro for this (ad-)venture. We found a good team to execute the plan and wanted to retain operational control for as long as possible. We concluded that approaching Private Equity firms was not the right way forward for us—despite the fact that a number of Private Equity firms showed strong interest at a later stage.

Instead we decided to go the "family and friends" route for this fundraising activity. We did this knowing that if the plan failed—for whatever reason—there could be personal risks to our reputation. Given that the management team has over 40 years of combined experience in Russia, over 20 years of combined self-storage experience and would personally invest 1 million Euro, we felt comfortable with this strategy. Notably, we agreed on a one share, one vote arrangement whereby all investors have a clear say in the company's organizational matters. As non-management investors hold 5/6th of the company's shares, they actually *do*!

In October 2010 we signed the first lease agreement, for an 8,200 m2 site in Moscow. After installing the boxes, IT equipment and erecting a Sales office, we opened for business on 1 April 2011.

By early 2011, we raised 6 million Euro from 44 investors scattered around the globe. Nearly all the investors have some connection to one or more members of the management team. The largest is a seasoned small-company investor with a fantastic opening question: "Harry, since you're the main force behind this fundraising, how much are YOU investing?" He indicated that if the amount was limited, our discussion wouldn't last very long! Fortunately, my answer pleased him and the subsequent due diligence process was concluded satisfactorily.

Harry Harbers is Co-Founder & Non Executive Director of SafeSpace. www.safespace.ru

The Agile Enterprise

Roland Harwood

In recent years, we've seen the rise of agile software development—an iterative method for delivering projects in a highly flexible and interactive manner. This resonates strongly with some of the issues associated with open innovation, and requires a more flexible approach to innovating with partners by sharing risks and rewards. In this article, I aim to illustrate the connections between these two trends and hope to show what a truly agile enterprise might look like.

What is Agile Development?

Forward3D's Martin McNulty describes the principles underpinning Agile Development in a recent Management Today webinar:

- Break down any big task into numerous small daily tasks.

- Prioritize the tasks and tackle them in order

- Ideally, allocate just one task to one person at a time

- Kill projects quickly if they aren't working—fail fast and cheap

- Aim for daily interaction with the project team members

It all sounds so simple.

What's the big idea?

All organizations want to innovate, but most of them don't know what that actually entails. Senior executives in many organizations often look for the next Big Idea—a new strategy or initiative. Yet this strategy is often dangerous because, as Nicholas Taleb argues in his book *The Black Swan*, we're bad at prediction and often what impacts us most is never foreseen. So the best approach to innovation is to seek agility; the principles above are a nice place to start.

Towards an agile enterprise

Henry Chesborough first coined the term open innovation; one of his most powerful examples of open innovation in practice comes from the film industry, where groups of actors, directors, crew and other freelancers coalesce for a period of time to innovate/create a new film and then disperse once the project is completed.

It may not be perfect but it's significantly different from the rigid organizational model most companies apply. The major benefit of this agility is that it only uses resources for as long as they're needed. Of course, the major weakness is that there's no organized learning structure. In fact, any new knowledge remains inside the participants' heads (though I'd argue that's often the case in organizations, too).

Everything big starts small

Many small- and web-based businesses, such as 100%Open are essentially agile in that they're almost entirely virtual, with minimal overhead and fixed assets. Many don't have employees but use a large network of freelancers, agencies and partners who work together to deliver projects. Many of these businesses don't have an office, but utilize a network of locations for hosting meetings. Finally, it's increasingly possible to have no fixed IT infrastructure, but instead use tools such as Basecamp, Skype, Google Apps, Crunch, Eventbrite, WordPress, and others via cloud computing.

It's exciting that the tools are all there in a way that they simply weren't a few years ago. Integrating all of these components is still challenging, yet it's not nearly as hard as it might seem and is certainly a far more efficient way to work.

Open innovation is increasingly becoming a smart strategy for big companies like IBM, LEGO and Procter and Gamble—but what about small companies? In many ways small companies are much more agile and adhere to the principles of open innovation constantly, because they have to be responsive to survive. Open innovation should never be seen as a strategic silver bullet, but rather a series of agile behaviors that are more productive in a networked world.

Roland Harwood is co-founder of 100%Open. www.100open.com

The Worst Leads to the Best

Edward Hissink

Coca-Cola is a great-tasting soft drink. And even at 125 years old, with 1.6 billion servings a day, it's also a well-delivered innovation. It is unique, yet also just a drink. Now, what's the worst thing that can happen in the realm of drinks? The obvious answer is being thirsty without having something to drink! So the best strategy would be to always be the drink at hand. Global presence was the exact strategy that made Coke big. Besides unavailability, there are worse things that can happen; there's something to drink, but it tastes terrible! This is a more difficult situation to deal with, due to subjectivity. Things could get worse: What if people say it tastes great, but it actually doesn't? The answer to this worst-case scenario is that the drink should be real—that it's the real thing. What did Coke do? They made sure you could get a coke everywhere, and that it was sold as the real thing.

How about coffee? Douwe Egberts realized that a lot of coffee was being poured down the sink. Commercially one might think, so what? Volume is volume whether people drink it or not. But for a coffee maker, getting poured down the drain is—or at least should be—the worst that can happen. Throwing something away because you don't like it is one thing, but throwing away something you actually enjoy is the worst. This led to Senseo—it had to.

Innovating for the sake of innovation won't get anyone anywhere. As Robert McKee, professor at the University of Southern California, succinctly points out, "Human nature is fundamentally conservative. We never do more than we have to, expend energy we don't have to, take any risks we don't have to, change if we don't have to. Why should we? Why do anything the hard way if we can get what we want the easy way?" What then will make an innovation come to life? The answer depends on the opposing force. What's the worst that can happen?

Your have a clear idea, the five W's of who, what, when, where and why are filled in, the concept has been tested, everyone involved has seen the prototype, top management buy-in is secured with a viable business model and you've got a strong team. Still, the journey from idea to realization is never an easy ride. The enthusiasm of the initial brainstorm, where a charismatic facilitator encouraged everybody to defer judgment, has long gone while the feeling of being asked to dance Swan Lake with your hands tied behind your back prevails. Remember that the single most important ingredient for any innovation to succeed is enthusiasm. Realize that resources—whether time, money or talent, and most likely all three—are always scarce and always will be. Deal with it. Start by recognizing and pinpointing barriers to overcome: both easily perceived practical barriers, and barriers that arise from thornier issues.

To bring potential barriers to the surface, start by asking all involved to answer the following questions anonymously: What obstacles do you expect to encounter on the journey towards the realization of value from the initial idea? What's your current biggest frustration? Read each other's blind and blunt responses during a workshop. Focus on identifying and removing obstacles, not killing messengers. Emphasize the importance of confronting the raised problems squarely and focus on going forward. Delve into the identified issues during the workshop with subgroups and report back with analysis. What are the opposing forces, what's the worst that can happen, what's the worst of the worst? And what's the best solution that will bring down the barrier? What do you need and what needs to be done? Dealing directly with uncomfortable situations requires stating them plainly, so there's no avoiding the challenge at hand.

A true challenge will awaken our inner hero. The more powerful and complex the opposing forces are, the better the innovation must become. Opposing forces must be overcome with authority. And innovating with authority brings authenticity, which in turn evokes emotion. The emotion that motivates people to make it happen, as well as the emotion people actually 'buy'. Only emotion is memorable and hence motivating. As Warren Beatty put it beautifully: "People will forget what I said, but they will never forget how I made them feel."

Edward Hissink is an innovation consultant at Brand Delivery, and has been involved in dozens of innovation projects at Sara Lee DE, Unilever, Akzo Nobel, KLM, AB Inbev, KPN, Nestlé, SAB Miller, HJ Heinz and Philips.

Innovation Delivery Is Mission Critical

Paul Hobcraft

Why is it that innovation seems to be incredibly rewarding for some firms, yet remains at best an unfulfilled promise for the majority? Why does innovation present such a stark and difficult choice for many, yet is so simple and successful for the few?

Is innovation such a mystery? The relationship between innovation efforts and its success lies increasingly in understanding the "go-to-market" phase—executing innovation delivery based on a clear grasp of the customer's needs.

The key to successful innovation isn't idea generation or putting all your creative efforts into the front end of innovation; ideas are always plentiful. It's turning this myriad of ideas into market or customer changing outcomes that deliver successfully based on understanding the customer's needs.

Unfortunately, there are no silver bullets for execution. For any established business, it means striving to perform above recognized standards. The ability to sustain leadership in the market is not just about the new product but also about its execution and delivery. You have to be ruthless to execute well in an unrelenting market, so make designated people accountable for meeting or exceeding standards. Normally, innovation delivery needs a highly engaged executive involvement. The innovation delivery part cannot be devolved, but must be well orchestrated.

Innovation always swims in uncertain waters. As uncertainty rises, the value of a well-considered strategy actually drops. Critical unknowns constantly arise; sometimes what you're left with as your innovation emerges becomes a starting point. Always be ready to adapt, be agile, be ready to experiment, explore and learn; failure to do so explains why execution is actually the harder end of the innovation process to get right. Everything hangs off a hypothesis and needs to be proven in its delivery. When innovation is at the heart of your strategy, you need to focus on and constantly review the best possible execution strategy.

Often the lack of a clear formalized decision making process for commercialization and going-to-market isn't there. Corporate leadership often leaves this to lower levels to execute, who struggle due to a lack of fact-based safety nets to manage the levels of uncertainty and are often reluctant to seek out leadership engagement to resolve conflicts. Far too often senior executives are engaged elsewhere and those left in charge of the execution process lack the courage to make often tough and game-changing decisions. This often damages optimal innovation delivery as teams often adopt "safety first" principles.

The ability to move an idea to implementation—with increasing agility—is what will distinguish a successful organization from a less successful one. The ability to execute well remains a critical performance gap, since innovation requires a deeply imbedded set of capabilities. Innovation is high maintenance—and high reward.

Increasingly complicated markets, the global pressures of consistent breakthrough and the additional emphasis on new business models cause escalating problems. Complexity at the innovation delivery stage calls for a higher level of organization, discipline and effective execution. This requires having the right capacity in place at the right time to drive execution through to its identified endpoints. Innovation delivery is where many decisions often get muddled through.

Clarifying and committing resources is a mission critical task. This is when you align your innovation process, organization, knowledge, technology, concept and performance with your go-to-market plans.

The considerations involved for effective innovation delivery lie around the following:

- Mapping and planning completely and thoroughly

- Building and editing based on changing insights
- Project management and planning
- Aligning and influencing multiple "vested" interests
- Collaborating with external stakeholders
- Bringing your diversity into a cohesive active and engaged participation

A g2m plan covers who, what, where and when and must include:

- Clarification of the needs and wants of customers in the launch.
- Attributes of success, a winning proposition articulated and constantly reviewed.
- A tight connection between innovation delivery and the whole innovation process
- A well thought through scope, timeline and approach to market strategy
- An honest definition of risks, economic, competitive and internal positions
- Realistic alignment capabilities and techniques and knowledge of the gaps to bridge
- The definition and clarity of the relevant value to the different parties and the final customer
- A clear value proposition that spells out the differentiation that is being provided by the new innovation and that keeps being referred to and evaluated
- An outline of the appropriate proof-of- innovation delivery concept (based on research, concept work, piloting, customer engagement, etc.)

- A plan to acknowledge and cultivate the critical relationships involved and make sure all parties are kept in the loop, with compromises only made to resolve impasse

- Clear ways of measuring the results, impact and success of a delivery

- The provision of feedback and enhancement opportunities/needs to all relevant parties, even back to the front end of idea creation to provide improved clarity and definition that helps

- A well-stated and well-managed clear accountability clarification of who does what.

Achieving correct, effective innovation delivery provides greater commercial success than simply allowing implementation to just happen as an afterthought.

Paul Hobcraft brings new forms of innovation competency into everyday thinking. www.AgilityInnovation.com, www.paul4innovating.com

Effective Launch Strategy

Erik Jan Hultink, Katrin Talke

The new-product development (NPD) process is regularly seen as a sequence of stages, which ultimately aims to present a new product to its target market and generate income from sales of that product. The launch stage encompasses all activities, facilitating an efficient diffusion of the new product in the marketplace.

Decisions made during the launch phase are recognized as important drivers of new-product performance. At the same time, new-product launch is often the single most costly step in the NPD process. Depending on the product and industry, this can include costs for mass-production, setting up the supply chain, establishing dealer and service networks, training the sales force, and advertising. The launch phase also involves great risk, as this stage is often the make-or-break point for a product's life cycle.

Launch managers are confronted with questions such as whether there will be a market apart from the initial innovators and technology enthusiasts, how competitors will react to the new product, how competition will evolve over time, whether the product functions will prove stable, and if the technology will become the dominant design. Owing not only to the importance of the launch stage, but also to the risks and significant commitments of time, money, and resources, formulating an effective launch strategy is a top priority for firms.

While strategic launch decisions are generally made in early stages of the NPD project, tactical launch decisions tend to occur at later stages after conceptual and physical development of the new product is complete. Most studies in this field define strategic launch decisions as comprising those decisions that set the parameters within which the new product will compete; that is, they define the objectives of the launch, select the market(s) where the product will be introduced, determine its competitive position and time the entry. Tactical launch decisions can still be modified at a later stage in the launch process and are mostly defined along the traditional elements of the marketing mix. Hence they encompass product, promotion, distribution, and pricing decisions such as the breadth of product versions launched, the nature and scope of services offered alongside the new product, how and where to distribute and promote the product, and its price.

From an aggregate perspective, launch performance usually requires setting clear, well-founded launch objectives, defining a precise target market, and positioning the product in a distinct manner. Significant investments in promotional and distribution expenditures also seem to drive launch performance.

It is argued that performance in launching a new product requires an analytical, risk-taking, and aggressive mind-set in order to be able to set clear and ambitious launch objectives and to proficiently make use of market segmentation and positioning. The results show that the dimensions of the corporate mind-set have a significant impact on most strategic launch decisions, which in turn significantly contribute to market performance.

Creating a marketing hype necessitates targeted interaction with relevant stakeholders such as dealers, suppliers, diffusion agents, and the general public to create a favorable atmosphere before the new product's launch. Sufficiently understanding the needs of all relevant stakeholders and addressing them in an adequate form are key.

Without compatible offers of complementary producers to add value, the attractiveness of the new product will decrease and the innovation may not become established as a standard. Without the support of sales agents, the new product's distribution may be endangered; and a lack of service offerings like consulting, training, or installation by adequate service providers can impede customer adoption.

A particular communication strategy relevant in the launch context is pre-announcement. Pre-announcements are pre-launch communication activities directed at market players—customers, distributors, suppliers, investors, and journalists—with the purpose of reducing uncertainty in the firm's favor. Generally, launch communication content can include three aspects of information: usability, technical and financial. Both usability and financial information have been found to be effective in improving market performance, while technical information is counter-effective.

The firm's frontline personnel can be seen as the first stakeholder group that needs to be won over to optimize launch performance. When given feedback on past performance, salespeople not only perform better, but can also be reminded of the results that they're expected to attain. As a result, they may feel less ambivalent about their role, and will be better armed to experiment and take risks in selling the new product. This finding suggests that if salespeople are rewarded on the basis of their outputs, they'll perform better.

Erik Jan Hultink is a professor of new product marketing in the Faculty of Industrial Design Engineering at Delft University of Technology.

Katrin Talke is a professor of entrepreneurship and innovation at Hamburg University.

Role of Entrepreneur Disappears from Large Organizations

Quintijn Innikel

The problem with most companies today is that they've been designed and honed to do just one thing. They've become well-oiled machines with small gears that precisely deliver that one perfect product. Companies have gone through lots of reorganization to rationalize their core processes, dedicating the best people for that well-defined, limited task in the greater scheme. This was done for a perfectly good reason: survival.

The downside is that within most corporations, responsibilities have been reduced to small packages of tasks and the walls between departments have become rock solid. Somewhere in the process the role of entrepreneur has disappeared, or is at best in the hands of the CEO.

When looking at these honed machines, it isn't hard to see where corporations struggle with delivering innovation. Innovation is, at its core, an entrepreneurial activity; passionately searching for ways to win consumers' hearts with superior products. Innovation is at its best where visionary marketers meet creative developers. That's unlikely to happen in this instance.

In our daily practice of helping companies with organizing innovation, we see marketers responsible for innovation struggle within their own department. Trying to discern consumer desire through market research is mystically called "insights", yet consumers are often clueless about what they want next. Isn't that the marketer's job to know? At best, this method will optimize products, give them better features or improve performance, but will never lead to breakthrough innovation.

On the other side of the wall, developers are frantically busy upgrading the company's current products. With detailed schedules on improvements, increased performance, revisions and redesigns, they hardly have the time and focus to step back and see what the next great thing could be. The R&D director usually sets the targets, and unsurprisingly 90% of these targets are technologically driven. They're not necessarily trying to serve their consumers better.

In this setting, marketers and developers commonly fight rather than create. Typically marketers feel they have specified in perfect detail what they want and when they want it, but their development colleagues just raise more questions, say it can't be done or take ages to deliver. From the developers' point of view, however, marketers keep coming up with fantasy propositions of brilliant, spec-loaded products for half the price of the competition. Sure, it would sell—but realistically it can't be made. In this setting, there's very limited understanding of each other's worlds and little respect for each other's work. In the meantime, companies with well-organized innovation will steadily increase their market share with superlative products.

With all this in mind, what's the best way to organize innovation? Both literature and company practice show a variety of solutions—Friday afternoon projects, incubators, dedicated innovation teams and venturing. Whatever shape it takes, innovation must start with vision and creativity. It must be an inspiring place in the company where marketers and developers meet, where ideas come to life in a workshop for prototypes, where all disciplines work jointly on new ventures—not just in those few hours a week they can spare for a project but in a truly dedicated way. Innovation is where developers truly listen to what their colleagues have to offer and where marketers must make choices and set priorities. This is where dreams meet reality.

In short, it's where true entrepreneurship is brought back to the heart of the company.

Quintijn Innikel is partner at Beacon Partners and helps in delivering product innovations for clients like Sara Lee, Danone, Atag, Heineken, Shell, Unilever and Bugaboo.www.beaconpartners.nl

From Imagination to Impact

Paul Isherwood

Over a century ago, Thomas Alva Edison had the foresight and energy to manufacture, market and deliver all aspects of his inventions. He truly believed that the real innovation challenge lay beyond the idea and famously summed it up: "Genius is one percent inspiration, ninety-nine percent perspiration." Without the processes and supporting culture that emphasize execution there is no true innovation, as no customer value is being created.

It's currently fashionable in many companies to focus on the supply side of innovation and come up with those few big game-changing bets. I'd argue that this approach results in too many small ideas being generated and a loss of strategic focus. The flipside could be that it's an excellent way to ensure operating excellence by making some quick wins and constant improvements to existing products and processes.

Incremental and disruptive innovations must combine in a portfolio balanced by varying degrees of risk and returns. To successfully adopt a strategy of step change innovation, large organizations often work outside mainstream paradigms, require larger leaps of understanding, demand a new way of seeing the bigger picture and undergo considerable change in basic technologies and methods.

To consistently launch new groundbreaking products or services, there must first be absolute clarity on understanding what the consumer needs are coupled with a detailed knowledge of the proposed science or technology. Technical solutions will likely come from outside the normal range of contacts, so an extensive network of internal and external sources is required to develop the new radical innovation. Finally, to achieve lasting commercial success, an essential part of the implementation plan is translating the science into a consumer benefit by creating compelling tailored communication.

The bottleneck in the innovation value chain for many companies is the commercialization stage, which can be both time consuming and problematic.

By having people driven by organizational structure, behavioral and cultural elements in place internally, and having an appropriate choice of external partners through differing agreements, business models and relationships, this can be overcome. Innovation is primarily a people issue; it is the softer factors that are key to successful execution, as I will further elaborate.

Fusion fuels innovation, and it's important to recognize that connectivity between people can generate energy and passion. This can be achieved by co-locating your commercial and R&D teams together in an innovation hub, where the open workplace leads to a greater sharing of more innovative and relevant ideas. Effective organizational planning ensures that you have dedicated people responsible for front-end ideation and a separate team looking after the back-end implementation. The trick is to manage the transfer of knowledge and information gleaned at the appropriate business approval point in each project.

Collaboration usually has a specific purpose and can be quite directive, relying on a detailed knowledge of the capabilities, expertise and strengths of each partner. It generally sets out to address a previously identified problem and does not happen naturally; it needs hierarchies and planning. The different values, backgrounds and cultures of the two parties can cause problems, but with persistence, mutual trust will develop and the benefits of win-win opportunities can be identified and shared. Broadening your blue sky innovation partner activities to include co-branding, in-licensing, out-licensing, co-marketing, co-creation, re-badging, alliances, joint ventures, etc., will enable you to execute a breakthrough innovation that might otherwise have proven difficult within the confines of a traditional organization.

Finally, remember that in the literal sense "execution" can mean either complete or kill—this is equally applicable to projects. If you can't implement and launch a product then you must have a rapid and effective exit strategy.

Paul Isherwood is Director of Innovation, External Networks & Partnerships at GlaxoSmithKline Nutrition. www.gsk.com

Accelerating Innovation Through IP Monetization

Just Jansz

Speed is a key element of an effective innovation process from invention to market introduction, and generally gets a lot of attention. Fast market penetration is often equally important for durable success, yet is typically not made the priority that it deserves to be. The main reason for this is that fast and broad market penetration requires significant resources in terms of capital and people, often exceeding the capabilities of the inventor's organization. This is true for startups and more established companies alike. This is true today more than ever as major growth opportunities appear in the fast moving emerging markets—each with their own specific challenges.

Since in many cases it will may not be possible to penetrate global markets with a new product or process fast enough using only in-house resources, it makes sense to consider alternative growth strategies. One such strategy is to build a strong and smart global IP portfolio that includes key elements that aren't easily copied and can subsequently be monetized through licensing and selective partnerships.

In most cases, licensing lets one penetrate global markets much faster than through one's own investment and can be done on a regional basis or for specific markets only. Partnerships based on licensed technology allow more direct participation in fast growth, but require particular attention to partner selection and are more intensive in resources than straight licensing arrangements. Income from licensing can be used to speed up R&D, whereas feedback from licensees supports ongoing development and improvement.

A good example of an effective licensing strategy is found in the chemical industry. In the late 1980s Himont invented the then revolutionary Spheripol process for polypropylene (PP), and quickly realized that no single company would have enough resources to invest in new capacity to keep up with fast growing demand. The active global licensing strategy, in combination with ongoing development of the technology, has been successfully continued by its successor companies Montell, Basell and

LyondellBasell. Today Spheripol accounts for more than 30% of the globally installed PP production capacity of approximately 60 million tons per year.

Just Jansz is Director of Expertise Beyond Borders BV and former President of Technology at Basell and LyondellBasell.

Innovation in the Chemical Industry

Herman de Jongste

Innovation in the chemical industry is a dichotomy. There are continuous improvements to process designs and the latest technology is rapidly applied to measuring and control systems in an everlasting race to improve efficiency and reduce costs. On the other hand, the industry is deeply conservative. Unproven and untested technologies are reluctantly tried out for fear that failure might cost more than the advantages it was supposed to bring.

Major base petrochemical products have been around for a long time; very few products have been added to the list since the Second World War. The chemical industry's customer base is no different. Hanging on to age-old specifications for fear of making changes with perceived unknown results is rife in the industry.t

A clear example is when chemical products are supplied to the car manu-facturing industry. Hydraulic brake fluids have been deployed since the introduction of hydraulic brake systems right after the First World War. The hydraulic fluid transfers the pressure on the brake pedal to four brake calipers, each in turn activating the brake shoe to the disc. The volume of less than a liter per car and associated cost are insignificant, yet the performance is crucial. Can you imagine how reluctant car manufacturers are to depart from such a proven system? For fear of lawsuits due to new design failure, the car industry only introduces changes after long and costly testing programs. When electronic brake systems were developed, brake system innovation was thought to be around the corner. Instead of using hydraulic fluid, the brake shoes are electrically controlled. This "brake by wire" concept is already long in use in the aviation industry. Modern aircraft use electric brake systems rather than hydraulic systems, but they serve a very particular purpose on the runway.

In the industry, innovation must go hand in hand with the old saying, "show me the money". Unless there's a clear economic benefit, very few innovations see the light of day. In the case of brake fluids, the risk of a recall and the added reputation loss has to be offset by savings. Not even superior products can swing the car industry to move to a different product. For this reason, the American car industry has adhered to a brake fluid formulation that has long been superseded. While car manufacturers in Europe have switched to a DOT4 (Department of Transport) standard, for fear of lawsuits the United States is sticking to a substandard DOT3 formulation.

How is this reluctance to accept innovation overcome? A continued accumulation of evidence that innovation is the way forward will help. The case must be stated at every opportunity, at trade fairs, scientific journals or industry publications, the process of attrition must be used to convince customers. Concentrate on one customer who is prepared (at huge effort and cost) to try the product. Once successful, others don't want to be seen as a "stick in the mud" and will eventually follow.

Herman de Jongste was responsible for part of the Chemicals portfolio of Shell Chemicals B.V., including Shell Brake Fluids.

Plea for Creativity as a Key Issue in Innovation Policies

Janjoost Jullens, Mattijs Taanman

The rules of the innovation game have gone through a major change in the past 20 years. Studies on innovation processes show that the linear innovation model doesn't help us understand why some innovations fail and others succeed. Innovation nowadays should be understood as a dynamic and ongoing process in which researchers, producers, consumers and policymakers interact, continuously reframe their expectations and redesign solutions in a changing context.

Against this background, the role of creativity as an intangible input with large economic and social value has become clearer and gained significant weight.

Creativity is currently the most important factor of production, even more so than labor and knowledge. Creativity determines which company wins the competitive battle, and the extent to which new knowledge leads to new economic activity in a particular sector. Although this validation of creativity isn't new, especially since policymakers worldwide read Richard Florida's *Rise of the Creative Class*, too many public and private decision makers hesitate to take the ultimate step. To truly match the needs of current innovation dynamics and the potential of creativity, creativity should be central and integral to the core of innovation policies. Instead, in many cases creative industries are set apart, focusing on the demands of sheltered prodigies instead of combining their expert values with other sectors.

The current Dutch innovation policy is a case in point. This policy has hallmarked the creative industry as one of the nine top sectors of The Netherlands's economic future. Amongst others, these top sectors include logistics, agrofood and life sciences. Each of the top sectors gets its own innovation policy, a public/private coproduction instigated by the Ministry of Economic Affairs, Agriculture and Innovation. Having great faith in the country's ability to think with imagination, we applaud the policy choice to include the creative industry in the top domain. A lot of potential can be realized there: with a 3% share in GDP that is steadily increasing, and a relatively high degree of innovativeness, the creative industry can be considered amongst the largest international economic catalysts. However, limiting the work field of 'creativity' to a specific industry or a sector doesn't do justice to either the creative professional or the potential that this sector entails. The standards must be raised.

This is where innovation dynamics kick in. As we know, the creative professional is more than an entrepreneur who merely creates jobs and produces GDP. The creative professional is above all a specialist, who not only offers technique (such as design), but is also an expert in precisely those domains innovation delivery so badly needs. Like no others, creative professionals are able to come up with new perspectives and ideas. Like no others, creative professionals give meaning and experience to ideas, products and processes and thereby mobilize people—consumers as well as project partners.

These skills are highly needed when reframing problems and opportunities, generating new paths of thinking, or bonding with new partners. These steps are taken constantly in the current multi-actor innovation processes, not only in the stages of inventing or design but also in the continuum of open innovation. This is why the number of creative professionals working in all of the sectors is likely a better determinant of economic growth than the size of the creative sector as a separate entity. Creativity isn't about one particular sector; it is the fuel for all innovations, from product development to societal innovation.

Therefore creative entrepreneurs should position themselves as valuable partners to other sectors, and in turn other sectors should invest in co-productions with creative partners. Policymakers need to invest in crossovers between the creative and other industries. For The Netherlands, the nine top sector action points that are now being formulated form the perfect place to start. Creative crossovers should play a role in each one of them. From knowledge through creativity to market: that's where our greatest economic potential lies.

Janjoost Jullens is connected to the Institute Societal Innovation and works part-time as a cultural entrepreneur in Rotterdam.
Mattijs Taanman is connected to the Institute Societal Innovation and is finishing his dissertation on the monitoring of innovation programs and processes at the Erasmus University.

The Power of Passion in Innovation

Peter Kapitein

Working toward better lives for people living with cancer and their loved ones is the mainstay of our mission. With every new step we take, our first concern is for the benefit to the patient.

Inspire2Live is an umbrella organization that coordinates a range of programs and events designed to accomplish our mission. What began as a joke in 2006 (cycling up mount Alpe d'Huez six times in one day) evolved over five years into an initiative with a 50 million Euro endowment earmarked for cancer-related research and applications, six events in Europe and the United States and a reliance on hundreds of volunteers that work with passion for patients and their loved ones. Besides these national events, Inspire2Live has set up a global initiative called "Understanding Life!" that brings together the best researchers and clinicians fully committed to getting cancer under control in ten years time.

Is this a simple goal? Absolutely, even though what needs to be done isn't always equally easy. But "Never Ever Quit" being our motto, we know one thing for sure: on January 17, 2021, cancer will be under control and people will be living happy and healthy lives in harmony with cancer.

The patient leads in everything we do. We set up projects and activities with and around the patient. We take this approach to our events, research projects and treatment programs. Whatever we do, it's always a joint venture between patients, researchers and clinicians—but patients come first! We connect the three groups, asking each to give the best they have plus some. We always do this independently; while aware of all the systems we deal with, we make sure we'll never become part of them. By steering this course we can make choices for the benefit of the patient in every circumstance.

Is this only possible for companies specializing in cancer care? Of course not. The principles of our initiative are simple and can work for any organization:

- Always explain why you do the things you do, not just what you do. People don't buy what you do; they buy why you are doing it. Remember that the what and the how are always debatable, but that the why never is. And there's always a why in every company. Most of the time this gets forgotten—but believe me, it's true.

- Take Mahatma Gandhi's words to heart: you must be the change you want to see in the world. If you want to achieve something, take the first step yourself and see how others respond. Then you take the second step, probably with one or two other people who have joined in to help you. Because once they see why you do it, they can help you with the how and the what.

- Use as few rules as possible and ensure that responsibility is borne at every organizational level, right down to the lowest. More rules leads to less thinking. Most of your employees know how things should be done better than you do, but you understand why things have to be done. Most employees like to take responsibility, so give it to them and enjoy an empty agenda.

We organized Inspire2Live, the events and the program "Understanding Life!" along the lines of these principles. The most essential part of it all is of course the passion that everyone who works in our organization brings— passion for the patients and their loved ones. And we combine this with our strong motto "Never Ever Quit"! When faced with disappointment or failure, we allow ourselves only five seconds of sorrow and then ask ourselves what we can do to make the situation a success. Complaining is useless. We don't ever want to be in a position where we have to explain to a patient that we couldn't help him or her because of problems that we couldn't solve. Don't just search for a solution...find it! Always be aware of the most urgent question in life, as Martin Luther King once asked: What do you do for other people?

In the coming years, we'll take the next steps. We'll set up over 20 PR and awareness-enhancing events across the world and will raise more than 250 million Euro per year, if not more. But the most important goal to meet is that people will lead happy and healthy lives in harmony with cancer together with their loved ones. Because the essence of life is living together.

Peter Kapitein is President and Patient Advocate of Inspire2Live.

The Sin of Objectivity

Gerry Katz

Why do so many great new product ideas never make it to market? Surely there are many reasons, but one particular story sticks in my mind as an explanation.

In the mid-1990s, I worked with a man who spent much of his career in new product development at Digital Equipment, the famous minicomputer manufacturer. In the late 1980s they had sent him to Japan for six months to work in a local business unit. Since this was the era when "Japan Inc." could do no wrong, I asked him what the biggest contrast between Digital Equipment there versus here in the West was. His answer was striking, and one that I'll never forget.

Every new product proposal at Digital Equipment was required to include a detailed financial pro forma, a common practice almost everywhere. In the United States, he said, that pro forma ruled. If the idea didn't look like it could turn a profit within a reasonable time then the project was killed, regardless of whatever other merits it might possess. In Japan, new product ideas were more likely to be evaluated based on their ability to address important unmet customer needs.

Anyone who has ever written an initial business plan for a new product knows that the financial numbers are pure fiction! Until the project has moved fairly far along in its development, it is almost impossible to forecast accurate sales and costs. So the practice of killing projects based on financial estimates at such an early stage in the process is almost ridiculous.

To him, the Japanese practice of focusing on the product's ability to satisfy the customer made a lot more sense. Of course the financials are important, but their philosophy was that if the product addressed an important customerneed, it would gain enough initial revenue to sustain the project for a year or two. During that time, the company would find ways to engineer costs out of the system to find a way to make it profitable.

That is why, to this day, I urge people to include representatives from finance on their cross-functional teams so that they can see the motivation behind the project and will become equally invested in its success. There is no greater sin than to kill a good project using seemingly "objective" financial criteria.

Gerry Katz works for Applied Marketing Science, Inc.

Speed Is of the Essence!

Jeroen de Kempenaer

New product development can be done quickly—perhaps it should always be done quickly. Not with undue haste, but as rapidly as possible. The following innovation project example took place in Singapore, at the Heineken joint venture brewery where I was the local brewmaster.

One early June, the management team of Asia Pacific Breweries (APB) discussed its portfolio of products and the increasing competition from imported beers; high priced "foreign", fancy products. APB had a range of products from the light tasting, low-alcohol Raffles, to the very strong ABC Stout. We needed a new special product to counter the importers. Chinese sales management was playing with the idea of light taste/high alcohol, but even in Singapore that was frowned upon. I suggested making a special beer with more flavor and the same alcohol content as our flagship Tiger beer. I promised a beautiful reddish golden color and fine taste. To my surprise, I got free reign and an unlimited budget, but the hard deadline of a full product launch by December 1st. Yes, that same year! December and the subsequent Chinese New Year account for about 30% of annual turnover, so a speedy launch would bring in a lot of money.

I contacted the Heineken pilot plant in The Netherlands asking them if they could make trial brews for us. They responded yes, next year around April I would be the first in line. My Chinese boss was not amused. He asked if we could try a DIY. Young and stupid as I was, I said: "Of course! We have a brewery and I'm a brewmaster. Let's do it!" It was a brewer's dream come true, to develop a new product all by oneself.

We flew in a special Crystal malt from Australia at 600% of the normal transport cost, but available within two weeks instead of seven. I used a classic old German recipe and by the end of June we made our first brew. A few weeks later the first version of Tiger Classic was ready for tasting. Normal market testing of a new product is costly and time consuming, and very often inconclusive. We decided to do this in a new way. Nobody knew the product, and it wasn't poisonous or anything; it just had a different taste and color. Everybody in marketing and sales got ten unmarked bottles and were asked to let their friends sample our new brew. We insisted that they only bring back negative remarks, like "This beer reminds me of my mother-in-law!" Not one negative review came back to us! Of course we'd fine-tune the taste on the way, but our new product was appreciated!

Subsequently, we made decisions on branding, pricing and labeling. We decided to go for a 30% premium on top of the already comfortable price level of Tiger. We launched our product in late November to a 3% market share; not hugely impressive but nice, at a very CFO-friendly price, and causing our importing competitors no end of annoyance! For all our haste and seemingly unlimited budget, we actually spent very little. There was no time for lengthy and costly (in)decisions and re-trials. In 14 days, we recouped all the project costs and started earning money with Tiger Classic.

Doing it quickly proved to be a very good choice, but not really the Heineken way of operating. Unsurprisingly, they went ballistic when I sent in the recipe for Tiger Classic. They definitely didn't appreciate that Heineken technologists had zero involvement. I simplified matters by leaving the company—I was already hooked on fast innovation and new product development.

Jeroen de Kempenaer is an ex-brewmaster and innovator. www.TheBridge.nl

Innovation Delivery Through Entrepreneurship

Paul Keursten

In today's world, with all its social, economical and environmental challenges, knowledge is the primary source of innovation, sustainable value and wealth. We need creative thinking and approaches, because "more of the same" won't create the sustainable solutions our world needs. The development and productive use of knowledge is becoming the key process of value creation for organizations as well as societies.

This fact changes the nature of work, organizations and the role of workers; work is becoming knowledge work, done by autonomous professionals working in networks where relationships are based on reciprocal appeal. The autonomous professionals are driving innovation and success.

They will only take this role seriously if they can act as entrepreneurs, working from their personal drive and talents, being free to take initiative and having the responsibility to develop themselves. They need to create what they see as valuable, and be able to co-create a context that enables them to do this.

Loyalty, obedience and compliance used to be core values in the industrial economy. In today's knowledge economy, these values lead to mediocre results. Passion, talent, creativity, freedom and responsibility are now needed for excellence.

Sustainable value lies in the ability to innovate
Any specific innovation or improvement has temporary value, but sustainable value lies in the ability to keep improving and innovating. A sustainable organization has the ability to identify, gather and interpret relevant information, to use this information to develop new skills, and to apply these skills to improve and radically innovate operating procedures, products and services. Learning lies at the heart of this process; both tracing relevant information and developing and applying new competencies are based on powerful learning processes. Yet you cannot go to a training course or formal school to develop the capability to innovate, where the

process and outcome are predictable and set by others. It requires individual and collective learning processes that get integrated in daily practice, where working and learning are one, where personal passion and curiosity perpetuate learning, and where there's a social climate of respect, support, feedback, sharing and caring.

Individual passion and talent is the main source
The process of innovation through knowledge productivity is a creative one, driven by human intelligence, knowledge, passion and imagination. This puts the human individual at the heart of organizing, and this applies to more than just a few highly talented people at the top. The number of creative professionals is rapidly growing, already making up more than one-third of the working population in developed countries and responsible for more than 50% of the total productivity. This demands courage, entrepreneurship, emancipation and passion. Conformism, loyalty and obedience—the carriers of the traditional economy—will not take us very far in the current knowledge economy or in solving the challenges of our world.

Individuals connect and make a difference through global networks
Individuals are operating in networks on a global scale, and globalization is taking on an individual level. Individuals have worldwide access to information, and people can share their ideas and products with the world. Space and markets are no longer local; social and economic activity transcends national and regional borders. The national market economy is changing into a worldwide network economy. In a network economy, access and participation take the place of selling and buying, cooperation based on reciprocal appeal and trust take the place of competition and conflict, and common interest replaces individual interest.

The central role of individual autonomy and entrepreneurship
When we acknowledge that knowledge work is growing in importance, that this type of work provides and demands continuous learning and that individual passion, talent, creativity and connections are driving

excellence in this work, we realize that our focus must shift toward the individual and start building strong and sustainable organizations around autonomous professionals. These are individuals who contribute to innovation and improvements, who are aware of their talents and contribution and continuously develop them, who insist upon autonomy, responsibility, and influence, who place high demands on their work environment, and who create opportunities for themselves and for others.

Autonomous professionals are entrepreneurs of their own talent, network and work, not employees following instructions. Their combined initiatives are the source of innovation and value. They're not interested in following the rules, but are prepared to break rules in order to create better futures for themselves and others. Their sometimes unorthodox, disturbing behavior should be seen as part of a solution instead of a problem. Let's build on these people, support and facilitate them, connect them with places and people that matter. We'll be fascinated by the results!

Paul Keursten works with Kessels & Smit, The Learning Company.

Innovation Delivery and Creativity

Nabil Khayyat

Ten years ago, capital and tangible assets were the main factors of production. You could buy a turnkey technology and have a business success. This was the Industrial Society.

The future, however, depends on the Knowledge Society; it is manifested by the volume, speed and ubiquity in generating scientific information and immediately applying that information to technological change. We are facing new challenges, opportunities and possibilities for using scientific knowledge and technology to achieve differentiation and increase competitiveness. We need the intensive application of knowledge in order to produce innovation.

Today most innovations are incremental innovations, not originals that lead to a first conclusion. We are too shy and comfortable. Shouldn't we *do* something? We are living in a moment of technological necessity. In today's fast moving markets, this necessity has shortened the average life of products. Companies have to respond rapidly to compete and even to survive—and their response must be based on innovation.

Although most members and managers recognize that innovation is crucial, not everyone knows how to implement it, others don't make it top priority and, most strikingly, those who hold innovation don't give it the importance it deserves. The current challenge is to innovate more rapidly and systematically. If we take a panoramic view of innovation, we see it as a way of valuing ideas, transforming creative solutions, applying products and processes that facilitate market access, and creating solutions that allow us to generate profits. To convert knowledge into innovative products and services—in other words, to make a shift from creativity to viability—we need to apply a number of advanced quality techniques:

- Quality Function Deployment (QFD): working on defining a new product (mature ideas) to reduce design time and costs in subsequent amendments

- Modal Analysis of Failures and Effects (MAFE): detecting and preventing defects from the design phase.

- Benchmarking: taking quality as an alternative and comparing with the best

- Co-makership: collaborating in production and following a new philosophy of supply

- Re-engineering: taking on the logistics and computerization of administrative, management, production and distribution tasks

This sort of innovation should be incorporated into business strategy, be treated systematically, and become part of the daily work in an organization. Innovation is complex and diversified; there are several factors that interact and promote the generation and commercialization of knowledge, products and services.

Nabil Khayyat is Head of Technological Division, Directorate of Evaluation of Life Science and Materials for Centre for the Development of Industrial Technology CDTI.

It's the Experience, Stupid!

Erik Kiaer

One of our clients was trying to reinvigorate its building materials business in a recent project. The initial work focus centered on potential levers for innovation. The executives considered developing a more flexible manufacturing process, or possibly increasing the effectiveness of their distributors, or even reducing package sizes if that might meaningfully change the economics of their business. They argued that growth had to come through the existing business system. It was entirely rational, yet it entirely missed the mark.

In taking this focus, the executives were more concerned about their own business practices and not thinking about why people bought their products. It wasn't because customers woke up in the morning with a burning desire to buy lumber, but because a homeowner dreamed of achieving a better life in a better home. By taking a step back, our client realized that the market didn't want hammers and nails; it wanted walls and rooms.

Once we defined this underlying motivation behind why people purchased building materials, the client understood that their real challenge wasn't about optimizing the existing distribution system. Their task was instead to build a network of architects and contractors who could deliver. By improving the homebuilding experience, our client could also unleash new demand and grow the overall market.

Making the switch from "Should we do this?" to "How can we make it happen?" can provide the defining moment of any innovation project. It's also the moment where many innovations founder. By focusing on what's practically achievable, or trying to predict possible profit in year five, clients regularly miss the ability to deliver a new, improved experience—and lasting growth.

One way to facilitate innovation delivery is to develop what we at Doblin call a business concept illustration. This can be anything from a simple sales brochure to a prototype store. The common element is that it immediately evokes an emotional response. Unlike "looks-like" or "works-like" prototypes, these illustrations aim to bring to life a fundamental shift in how the innovation addresses a market need. This isn't about asking our clients to "imagine a world where..." or suspend disbelief. Rather, it makes the new idea hook into everything we already know to be true, showing how magical a new experience might be.

Teams have to focus on this element of magic in order to help sponsors understand why the innovation is important. If teams can express how their project will meaningfully change an experience, financial analysis becomes less of a focus. Given that it's often a fool's errand to try and predict innovation using most common metrics, this is incredibly useful.

For our building materials client, we didn't focus our business concept illustration on the contractors who bought and used the product. Instead we focused on the housewife who dreamed of a home—our client's clients' client. We developed a short animation describing how they can help the housewife achieve her dream. They knew they could help her; they just never realized she was part of their business equation. In a four-minute video, we were able to turn them from being skeptical about why they should invest to instead asking us how they could accelerate development.

Erik Kiaer is account leader and associate partner with Doblin, a member of Monitor Group. www.doblin.com

Healthy Future by Easy Allotments

Ditmar Koster

A healthy future starts with healthy nutrition. On average, one in seven boys and one in six girls in the Netherlands are overweight; in large cities this figure is much higher, with as many as one in three children being overweight in some districts. Excess weight not only leads to problems for the children suffering from it, it also incurs substantial healthcare costs. The total costs to society caused by being overweight or obese are currently at least 3.2 billion Euro per year. Recent studies demonstrate that investing in a preventative approach focused on a healthy lifestyle pays off both socially and economically. People who learn unhealthy eating and exercise habits at an early age have difficulty adopting a healthier lifestyle in later life. Therefore it's key that both children and their parents learn to keep an eye on their energy balance from a young age. (See the 2009 policy document on being overweight.)

The majority of interventions for children regarding healthy weight take place when they are primary-school age or older. Relatively little attention is paid to children in the 0-4 age group, despite the fact that a healthy future starts with healthy eating habits learnt at as young an age as possible. For example, eating vegetables is a key feature of such healthy eating habits, yet dietary surveys among young children demonstrate that the intake of vegetables by 18-month-old, 2-year-old and 3-year-old children leaves much to be desired. In addition to essential vitamins and minerals, vegetables also provide dietary fiber and are low in energy, making them a fundamental component of a daily diet.

Children aged 0-4 and their parents or guardians can easily be reached at playgroups and nursery schools. Our aim therefore is to raise awareness of the value of vegetables and the importance of healthy eating habits in children under four among children, parents and teaching staff at these institutions. The information will be communicated interactively and according to the needs and interests of the target groups.

As national partner of the Unit for Youth at a Healthy Weight (www.jongerenopgezondgewicht.nl), Nutricia Nederland B.V. was the driving force behind the public-private partnership between the Municipality of Utrecht, Cumulus Welzijn, Ludens and Aveant as well as the Municipality of Rotterdam, Prokino and Kinderdam. It formulated a joint approach to implement the pilot project Easy Allotment Gardening for Preschoolers in the municipalities of Utrecht and Rotterdam. This local approach responds very specifically to the target groups' needs and reference points, bearing in mind that the problems and approach needed may differ between districts and target groups.

The project is dedicated to setting up Easy Allotments at approximately 30 nursery schools in Utrecht and 17 in Rotterdam. By means of the allotments themselves and the related teaching, the preschoolers learn in a fun way about the "ground-to-table" journey taken by vegetables. Workshops on healthy nutrition for preschoolers are organized for parents and the teaching staff of the nursery schools and playgroups in order to broaden their knowledge. Group activities organized with the children will give both preschoolers and their parents the opportunity to discover that vegetables are fun, delicious and incredibly healthy.

The Easy Allotment gardening project includes the following components: social marketing, partnership between public and private parties, the provision of information about healthy nutrition for teaching staff and parents, educational resources for preschoolers, and educational resources and instructions for nursery and playgroup staff.

The public/private partnership will be further developed in the near future. Nutricia will help create training and employment opportunities to sustain this Easy Allotments initiative. In doing so, it will bring together various parties to share specific knowledge and insights based on years of research, and actively support this initiative through its staff and other stakeholders.

Ditmar Koster is General Manager of Nutricia Nederland and a member of Groupe Danone. www.nutricia.com

Be Like a Radar

Rogier and Roland van Kralingen

However different they may be from one another, the most successful innovations on the planet are similar in that they strike the right chord at the right moment in time.

Our definition of innovation is very simple: innovation is synonymous to added value. Something needs to be relevant and different in order to add value. In the commoditized markets of today, functional innovation is often not enough; brands, products, museums, events, services, buildings and people need to make emotional connections.

This isn't easy. Innovation speed is crucial in these times of rapid commoditization, which is why companies often turn innovation into a process. This professionalization has not necessarily led to better innovation results, however.

The most important reason for this failure is because these processes are focused on the competences of the company itself, not on what we call connectivity, or being connected to all relevant developments in your companies' context. Companies tend to look internally for optimization, efficiency and best practices. The focus on this internal process can benefit the company in the short term, but it says nothing about the long-term position of a company on the market.

Most companies point to their market research partner for connectivity. Yet however useful market research can be, by its very nature it only reports the status quo, while the most important trait a true innovator has is curiosity, the ability to go out and experience or discover things themselves.

Innovation is more than a company process; it is a state of mind, or in some cases even a way of life. It must be done with your own hands. It means every morning we must listen to the radio station of our target group while we drive to work, read their favorite magazines, try to get the editors of those magazines drunk so they expose their secrets to your market, do a

Hot Product Scan© for brilliant new ideas on the Internet, do a Hot Concept Tour© of the best retail shops, take a Consumer Safari into the consumer jungle and actually talk to people, memorize the ten best books and articles in your field of work, have a deep understanding of the emotions of your target group, give space to the misfits in your office and get everyone on the work floor involved in the creative innovation process through leading by example.

Being connected greatly increases the chances of successful innovation. Connectivity means better ideas, more involvement and better innovation realization in the end. Such an open-minded approach to innovation is something rarely found in most businesses. Those companies that wish to add relevant and distinctive value have to open their doors and windows for a fresh breath of innovation air. Innovation is out there on the streets, not in the office. If you wish to be a successful innovator, you need to turn your company into a "radar station", picking up all relevant bips and beeps in the surrounding context. We always tell our clients: Be like radar.

One of the top examples of innovation realization is the story of iPod & iTunes. The reason the iPod is such a strong example for successful innovation is because Apple was well connected to the developments in their respective context.

The market for portable music equipment used to be dominated by the Sony Discman CD Player. But Sony didn't see the mp3 audio encryption technology (from the German Frauenhofer Institute) appear on their radar, nor did they see that in the space of only months, teenagers everywhere were switching to mp3 for their musical needs.

Apple was awake, however. They borrowed/copied mp3 player interface technology from sound hardware manufacturer Creative and added a good deal of emotional design to create the look of the mp3 player. Their biggest masterstroke was the distribution software iTunes, which created a digital environment separate from the regular Internet, and is now used for iPhone, iPad and the App Store. By being so connected, Apple created an immense amount of added value, surpassing their competitors with apparent ease.

Rogier and Roland van Kralingen *are authors of* De groeimotor (Growth Engine) *and* Emotionele Innovatie (Emotional Innovation) *as well as founders of Inncvation Consultancy INNOA. www.innoa.eu*

Focus on Minimizing Risks to Offer the Best Possible Solution to the Market

Rob Kuilboer

Research and innovation have been extremely important factors in Siemens' success from the company's start in 1847. The two are complementary: research transforms money into knowledge, while innovation transforms knowledge into money. Research is a necessary though insufficient pre-condition for innovation. Innovation is determined by the invention plus market success. Companies need to continuously create economic value, which can only be done by creating successful innovations. The business strategy drives the R&D strategy.

Siemens' innovation strategy is to be a pioneer in all our businesses (Energy, Industry, Healthcare and Infrastructures & Cities) to secure the most competitive edge. This strategy must be consistent in the following areas:

- Technology strategy, focusing on trendsetting technology portfolios and a leading position

- Patent strategy, by increasing patents in trendsetting technologies

- R&D resource strategy, by effective spending

- Processes/people/skills/culture; full leverage of our capabilities and assets to tap further potential

The innovation strategy depends on the business' position along the technology lifecycle (First Mover, Fast Follower, Trendsetter).

Siemens also possesses a great deal of insight about future trends. This has aided in the development of our unique procedure for future strategic planning—our "Pictures of the Future." Together with our various business units we continually study important trends, such as those related to the future of rail transport, sustainable energy supplies and affordable health-care systems.

Maximum performance with 50% less parts

When left on its own, complexity tends to increase in technology. So it was with Siemens' wind turbines. As a result, Siemens set about trying to deliberately shift the paradigm of wind turbine manufacturing from complex to simple. The project team in the engineering department was given a challenge: Create a powerful new wind turbine for the 2- to 5MW class market with 50% fewer parts than a 2.3MW machine, that's easy to transport, install and maintain.

After several years of preliminary research, it was concluded to be doable, and in late 2006 the development work was formalized as a concrete R&D project. The first results of the project were two SWT-3.6-107 wind turbines with a direct drive generator rather than a gearbox. By keeping all the components except the gearbox, the project team could accurately measure the effects of the new technology. In parallel with the testing of the first two wind turbines, the development of a cost-optimized direct drive turbine started up in 2008, which resulted in a newly erected prototype by early 2010.

With this turbine, Siemens Wind Power has developed an excellent and competitive product. Technically, the new direct drive wind turbine SWT-3.0-101 is robust: solid and simple solutions have a high priority. This wind turbine is easy to maintain and extremely reliable. The compact design also allows for cost-effective transportation and installation.

In the near future, we must focus on minimizing risks. Through testing and validation, we have to ensure that everything works as intended, as well as identify and eliminate all potential failures so we can offer the best possible result on the market. Another important task to be solved in cooperation with Supply Chain Management and Quality is preparing the turbine for serial production and building up the right processes and procedures.

Rob Kuilboer is a technical sales manager of wind turbines at Siemens. www.siemens.com/wind, www.siemens.com/innovation

A Degree of Protection Against the Ill Effects of Failure

Ulf Landegren

The process of innovation is often described as driven by observed unmet needs; at least this is seen as the ideal state of affairs. A brief look at successful innovation delivery results suggests a more complex picture. Many radically new innovations arise as observations of some interesting basic process that only later find applications for a useful purpose, often in a completely different area from where that idea first arose. On the other hand, a clear view of present or emerging market needs is obviously valuable when rummaging through stores of interesting procedures in search of ones that might address a perceived need for possible commercialization. Accordingly, innovations often come from a dynamic interplay between novel, abstracted basic research findings and a keen eye for solving important problems.

The view of innovation expressed above prompts questions about how to provide an optimal basis for innovations and quickly realize new concepts. The interplay between academic research and industrial application is particularly productive if the two areas can be brought to closely interact over many cycles of discovery and application, with mutual respect for the different competences the two parties bring to the table. Certain elements of the chain of innovation delivery are best conducted in an academic setting, while others need an industrial milieu.

Academic research has much to gain by encouraging its practitioners to take chances and perform experiments that could open new vistas, despite an uncertain chance of success. In this context an academic system dominated by delivery-driven research with strict goals and timelines can reduce innovation opportunities. We must also find ways to fund risky, failure-prone research alongside the steady march of "normal science", incrementally expanding knowledge. Moreover, we must offer young scientists a degree of protection against the ill effects of failure, perhaps by creating larger academic environments where risky and safer projects can be pursued in parallel.

Once promising applications with a potential commercial value have been identified, then the project must enter an entrepreneurial phase where work is pursued in an industrial setting. This can be achieved by licensing intellectual rights to existing industrial organizations. However, for highly promising and radically new technologies a startup may offer the best opportunity to realize the full value of the innovation. This phase of the innovation cycle is highly dependent on the availability of industrial expertise and networks, and on factors such as access to early economic support and possibly venture capital.

Working in Uppsala, Sweden, I am a beneficiary of the older academic system where academic scientists still control rights to their own inventions. This is a situation that is becoming rare internationally, but offers interesting opportunities and challenges for commercializing inventions.

Ulf Landegren works in the Department of Immunology, Genetics and Pathology at Uppsala University.
www.igp.uu.se

Flywheel Collaboration

Ton Langeler

There was excitement around the classroom. "It's like magic!" whispered the crowd. Seemingly nothing happens when some concentrated hydrogen peroxide is mixed with liquid soap. But when a catalyst is added, suddenly the hydrogen peroxide reacts much faster and delivers a thick bubbling foam. It looks like elephant toothpaste (Google it) but is nothing more than harmless oxygen and water.

A catalyst will increase the speed of the process, but can't replace any of the basic ingredients. The same is true for innovation; you need collaboration between technology and commerciality. At times this might look like a long process—try the "flywheel" catalyst to realize innovations fast and thick.

A large number of innovation efforts never become successful products or services. Instead of approaching an innovation process from a linear perspective, consider the process as a flywheel with a short, fast revolution. Such an approach can result in quicker and more sustainable innovation delivery.

In order to realize true innovation, it's essential to look beyond technical possibilities and beyond the demands of the user. Intensive and frequent evaluation and optimization of the demands and opportunities are needed. The Innovation Flywheel© advocates a short, fast cycle of enrichment. In just a few weeks all the value experts are consulted as to how the idea can best be realized. By applying a number of these short cycles, the innovation has a greater chance of success. All the experts, including the end user, are aligned and this interaction effectively creates added value. The revolution of the flywheel is repeated until it's spinning at full speed and a sustainable delivery of the idea is generated.

Value experts
The spokes of the flywheel each represent a value expert. Product Development is often undertaken by several departments and sometimes even by several companies. The Market is also usually divided into a number of parties, such as end user, buying agent and trade and/or supply chain.

All these parties add value to the innovation and are therefore defined as value experts. The chance of market success is much larger if these different value experts are closely connected.

Product concept

The axis of the flywheel is the letter C for concept, a pre-defined product concept. The concept is the center of the Flywheel and thus the gravitational center of the whole innovation delivery process. A product idea (by way of the fuzzy front-end of innovation) or a technological solution (from a lab) will need to be verified by the user and translated into a pre-defined concept. By placing such a concept at the center, the front-end and the back-end or delivery stage are continually linked and customer demand is anchored in the base of the process. By doing this, we can produce better insights and more successful innovations.

Iterate

Each connection with a spoke in the flywheel can be seen as a step in the process, falling under the responsibility of a particular department. Each stage can now be precisely defined, and after each revolution the organization can decide if they want to get the next revolution going. The penultimate revolution of the flywheel will end by introducing the new product to the market. What then follows is one last vital revolution, namely market optimization. Once this spin has been completed, the innovation can be passed on to the existing line organization.

At each revolution, each stage of development, we increasingly focus on the possibilities and demands and so continually work towards a new solution. This type of collaboration is far more interactive than that suggested by a linear Stage-Gate® Process. As Michael Polanyi, a twentieth century scientist, puts it, "all achievements of knowing involve creative and active integration".

A comprehensive front-end stage with adequate interaction will result in more in-depth insights into demands and possibilities, and consequently all the other aspects of the marketing mix. What's more, at each phase, we find out what the most appealing selling points are—information that can then be used by the sales team during the launch. Ultimately, successful innovation implementation results in more sales, increased customer satisfaction and even more sales. The flywheel gets to spin at full power and adds momentum to your growth.

Ton Langeler is the co-author of Innovatie uit de Polder *and founder of pro-Actuate Innovation Delivery Management.*

A Risk Worth Taking

Rob van Leen

In recent years, DSM has developed into a focused life sciences and materials sciences company, and currently puts innovation at the heart of everything it does. As part of this transformation into what we call an "intrinsically innovative company" we have thoroughly revised our strategy, structure and culture. Of course, we've also made inevitable mistakes along the way.

The hurdles we came up against related primarily to market developments or the composition of our innovation teams. We learned the hard way with market trends that were difficult to predict and hesitation when it came to taking advantage of potential new opportunities (including opportunities with customers). For example, with our project to develop transparent, high-vitamin milk we discovered that what the market wanted was something totally different from what we had expected—in fact the market has no interest in milk that has been "tampered with".

The second element relates to the composition of our innovation teams. Depending on which phase a project is in, the competencies and the behavior of the team members can have a decisive effect. An entrepreneur with vision and fearlessness who thrives on finding new ways to do things is a great asset during the startup phase of a project. In the later project phases of consolidation, scaling up and market introduction, stamina and specific management qualities are primary requisites. It's imperative to have the right person in the right place at the right time if your innovation process is to be a success—that too is a lesson we had to learn.

Focusing on innovation also means being prepared to take risks. Yet at the same time, there needs to be a balanced view of the market and technology. In the past, technology-driven companies have regularly been accused of not taking sufficient account of the market, which meant they came up with answers to questions that were never asked. A very important lesson learned here was that in the end it's the customer who determines whether or not an innovation is successful. Nevertheless, it can still be worth searching for new markets for a given technology, perhaps in combination with a review of the business model. For example, we developed a technology for resin-on-glass for a market that was of little interest to our existing business, and therefore we did not have the necessary sales or distribution channels for it. Thanks to its anti-reflective properties, this glass is suitable, amongst other things, for picture framing. We took it upon ourselves to produce and distribute the glass under the brand name Claryl®. After a hesitant start, this material is now being sold right across Europe and this year we are going to launch it onto the American market as well.

A stronger external focus is one of the cornerstones of DSM›s strategy, and a tightening of market focus has given rise to significant improvements. On the other hand, we know that fundamental breakthrough innovations are often technology-led, and that with the necessary perseverance a given technology can be matched with existing or latent market needs. Anyone who finds such a match should be proud of having been brave enough to take a calculated risk and to embark upon this search.

Rob van Leen is the Chief Innovation Officer for Royal DSM NV.

Getting Your People Ready for Innovation

Stefan Lindegaard

The leaders of successful small companies know how important it is to have the right people in the right position. When resources are slim, the ability of everyone to do their job well matters tremendously. One or two weak links can spell the difference between success and failure. So it will come as no surprise when I say that when it comes to making innovation of all types happen, people matter more than ideas.

Consider that many innovation initiatives fail because their leaders don't understand this simple fact. In fact, it is more important to have grade-A people than a slew of grade-A ideas. Why? Grade-A people can take a grade-B or perhaps even a grade-C idea and turn it into a successful reality. Grade-B people, on the other hand, struggle with even truly great ideas.

If we take this to the world of small business, the big question is whether there are enough Grade-A people within your organization who can take great ideas, whether they come from inside or outside the company, and make them real.

When large corporations tackle this question, their answer is simple: with a large body of employees, it's easy to switch great people to other projects. But for a small company with few staff members, the ability to do that doesn't exist. In this case, it is particularly crucial to identify and develop people with the attributes and skills needed to turn an idea into a finished product or service. Before you get all fired up about generating a ton of ideas, first figure out how you're going to match those ideas to people who can make things happen.

As you start this work, here's another key point to remember: The skills needed to lead and manage a project within the existing core business—where innovation is likely to be incremental and resources plentiful—are significantly different from the skills needed to overcome the challenges and obstacles that greet almost any new business project involving break-through or radical innovation. This is especially challenging in small companies where resources are hard to come by. You need to staff new business projects with people who have a mindset and toolbox to match this different challenge.

You also need different people for the different phases of the innovation process, which presents another challenge for small companies. Just as some entrepreneurs are better at running a company at its very early stage and others are better at helping the business scale once the product is launched, so, too, are there entrepreneurs who are better suited both in terms of mindset and skills to various phases of the innovation process.

For example, the discovery-innovation-acceleration (D-I-A) model of innovation put forward by the Radical Innovation Group identifies three phases of innovation:

Discovery
- Basic research: internal and external hunting.
- Creation, recognition, elaboration, and articulation of opportunities.

Incubation
- Application development: technical, market learning, market creation, and strategic domains.
- Evolve opportunities into business propositions: creating a working hypothesis about what the technology platform could enable in the market, what the market space will ultimately look like, and what the business model will be.

Acceleration
- Early market entry: focus, respond, and invest.
- Ramp up the fledgling business to a point where it can stand on its own, relative to other business platforms in the ultimate receiving unit.

This model has been used successfully at many companies, who have learned that very few people have the skills to move from heading the project in the discovery phase to heading it during the acceleration phase. The challenge this presents for small companies is obvious. With far fewer personnel to choose from, it's tough to fill all the slots identified in this model. The good thing is that you can identify people with the right mindset, and start working on their toolbox. Making people more prepared for innovation by continuously developing their toolbox is one of the lowest-hanging fruits, and this can be done in small as well as big companies.

Stefan Lindegaard is Founder & Chief Facilitator of 15inno.

Exploring Entrepreneurship

Mario Mahr Ávila

The three main pillars of knowledge capital are education, research and innovation. But are they sufficient to turn an idea into a successful reality and translate benefits to society? The answer seems to be no. It doesn't matter how large or how may support mechanisms are visible up on the "roof", they will not work if the "roots" are not adequately built to prompt the knowledge flow capillarity. Pumping knowledge from roots to the roof, from human capital to society, is the simple and risky work called entrepreneurship. The term has been used in multiple and diverse ways, but few really know how to use it to generate high and sustainable growth ecosystems. Entrepreneurship isn't just about receiving money for startups (roof); it also needs spirit and talent (roots) to flow accordingly. Its combination of art and science is profound.

It is an art, or spirit, that emerges thanks to the inspiration, creativity and added value that motivates individuals to generate unique attitudes and behaviors. It supposes an inner cultural challenge that presently differentiates entrepreneurs with incremental or disruptive initiatives. Breakthrough innovations can emerge from provoking interdisciplinary cross-thinking, or even by provoking and exploring serendipitous events.

It is also a science, or talent, that structures the conditions and procedures to deliver and convert the spirit into talent. It basically supposes an outer contextual challenge that must meet certain measures and keep the spirit flowing through a coordinated framework of OECD-based structural determinants, such as smart regulation (usually evidence-based), capacities-building (such as mind-setting, absorptiveness, and competitive management), knowledge creation (with motivation incentives, collaboration, and protection), financing (early-stage matching), markets (including market entry), and culture (including culture change).

The key to creating a successful combination of art and science, and therefore delivering tangible benefits to society may depend firstly on building the individual and contextual conditions that permits entrepreneurs to launch innovative projects (a new species of fish, for example), not only by detecting the right idea (flying fish) within a huge and rapid competitiveness world (oceans and currents) but by managing the right moment (early in the morning), at the right place (Barbados), with the right resources (a fish caught while flying, using nets held from outrigger canoes).

If entrepreneurs detect good disrupting ideas but aren't conscious of its potentials, innovation will not be fruitful.

Mario Mahr Ávila is an EU Advisor.

Execute with Precision, Hard Work and Skillful Knowledge

Sriharsha and Satyanarayana Masabathula

The 21st Century heralds the advent of a new era in innovation, where ideas have to be intertwined with management in order to attain goals. They must be executed not only with precision and hard work, but also with skillful knowledge management. Using ideas effectively is the key to successful innovation delivery.

VEDA Climate Change Solutions Limited (VCCSL), promoted by Vanitha Empowerment, Development and Advancement Mutually Aided Cooperative Society (VEDA MACS) Ltd., is a Knowledge Processing Organization established in 2005 to connect the rural poor to international carbon markets through global mechanisms such as United Nations Framework Convention on Climate Change (UNFCCC). It aims to integrate carbon finance with povertyalleviation in the most backward regions of India using appropriate Afforestation and Reforestation (A/R) practices. The idea is to maximize stakeholder profits through "unusual business". As we await the first release of carbon revenue to the farmers before the end of 2011 with bated breath, the journey to this milestone—to deliver our innovation—has been a daunting task. There were two main challenges that we'd like to share with you here.

Probably the most arduous challenge that we faced along this journey was making poor and illiterate farmers understand how they would benefit by participating in the project. It would be useless to try and explain to them the implications of climate change and how they could help mitigate it. The only part that would catch their attention is the promise of additional revenue from carbon credits that would help them put food on their plates. This gap between big ideas and material groundwork is where we believe most innovations lose their way. VCCSL's qualified team consists of idea generators as well as people who have worked with farmers on the ground for over 20 years. Together they helped create a small, intense environment that contributed to both ends of the spectrum, eliminating shortcomings that either of them might have overlooked.

Another interesting challenge we encountered during replication of the pilot project was in the species selection for generating carbon credits. The replication project was supported by the Rabo Foundation and developed by a nonprofit enviro-social enterprise (Socio-eCO2nomix-Global) promoted by VCCSL. During monitoring of the pilot BioCarbon Fund project with the World Bank, it was noted that species choice should have been left to the farmers' discretion. This would have given them the opportunity to plant trees that are more financially beneficial to them. It was wrongly assumed that the illiterate farmer was not aware of what may be best for him. In fact, despite their illiteracy the farmers were well aware of the market situation and were best placed to make the right choice. Drawing from this, Socio-eCO2nomix-Global presented the farmers with a broad species choice keeping in mind the associated environmental benefits that the project aimed to achieve. This open-minded approach, as opposed to imposing species by the paper industry on farmers, is central to successful innovation. This participatory process not only secured voluntary farmer involvement in the project but also helped the enterprise in its ground network through collaborations with local governmental and non-governmental organizations, strengthening the project in terms of sustainability.

Sriharsha Masabathula is the President of VEDA Climate Change Solutions Ltd. and is currently a student of Ohio Wesleyan University, USA.

Satyanarayana Masabathula is the Honorary Adviser for Socio-eCO2nomix-Global and VEDA Climate Change Solutions Ltd.

Teaching Elephants to Dance: Big Corporations Can Embrace Innovation

Chris Mason

"Skunkworks." "Mavericks." "The Pirates inside." Even "the crazy ones". These are just a few of the words and phrases that have been used to describe innovators and which indicate they are not people in the corporate mainstream. Over time, large organizations have struggled to reconcile the tension between two views of the world: the managerial one, the captains who want to steer a steady ship through the predictable, smooth, charted seas of quarterly earnings targets and the innovative one, pioneers for whom life is a voyage of exploration, discovery and perilous adventures in uncharted waters.

Yet both talents are necessary for success. Rationally, the managers know they need the innovators' fresh perspectives to stay competitive. Grudgingly, the innovators admit there's value to be had in streamlining, systemizing and developing their ideas over the long term.

So, why the struggle? Most CEOs in a recent BCG study on innovation cite "risk-averse culture" as their biggest barrier to extracting value from innovation. When the big boss wants innovation and sees risk aversion, what's gone wrong? Innovation disrupts the smooth operation that managers prize. It brings change in products, processes, and routes to market—that's a pain.

In our experience at Triniti Marketing, leading & embedding change in global clients, a methodical and sustained commitment is what's required. Innovation is no exception; dramatic improvements in client innovation capability are possible. One global client leapt 33 places in the international innovation rankings. But there is no silver bullet.

Clear, shared vision
The CEO's view alone is not enough. Often there are other leaders within the company who pay lip service to the need for innovation but whose every action sends a different signal. Is the innovation pipeline review the last item on the agenda after monthly sales? Are the rising stars working on innovation projects or managing the current business? At one company, it

wasn't until unambiguous share of sales from innovation targets were set and widely published that senior managers below the main board really started to take innovation seriously.

Changing organizational capability
Consider the skills and knowhow required to innovate successfully. If the organization is looking for breakthrough ideas, don't underestimate other capabilities that might be needed beyond the existing business model. The much lauded Nespresso system from Nestlé required retailing knowhow, Internet fulfillment and partnering with machine suppliers & CRM capability, most of which the business needed to acquire beyond its coffee technology core. You also need to pay attention to process. Many companies believe that a "funnel and gates" system is all they need to unleash the magic of innovation. But how is the funnel being fed with quality ideas? Are there more ideas waiting to be progressed so that existing failed projects can be culled with no one fearing for their job? When do the innovators find time to dream? Google is famous for allowing its engineers 20% time to pursue their own ideas beyond those projects they are formally tasked with. If your business believes the same people can both "manage" and "innovate", then there's a need to seriously think about the support required to prevent the managerial day job squeezing out all new possibilities.

Changing certain individual behaviors
One aspect we believe to be crucial is the need to structure and signpost interactions between managers and innovators. At certain points in an idea's life, a manager needs to nurture and give constructive feedback. However, unless that need is clearly signposted the idea gets "managed" along with everything else on the managerial agenda. Space has to be cleared for innovation discussion, and for the innovator to recognize they need to clearly signal they type of input they want. At the same time, we also want to ensure that the manager picks up the signal and understands that critical evaluation will be utterly necessary at a point later in the idea's life.

Plan and measure carefully

It's all about the proper sequence. We've learned to start with the leaders, working multi-functionally amongst both managers and innovators. Innovation can only be fostered when there is genuine top-level curiosity and desire to change the organization's pace & quality of innovation. People lower down have well-honed survival antenna, and will be looking for signs of dissent or division in the leadership. Innovation is messy and disruptive for managers, so any sign that the leaders don't really mean it will be leapt on enthusiastically. Setting and tracking measures are great ways to help the managers get on board. After all, hitting the numbers is what they do.

As Lou Gerstner from IBM asserted, elephants *can* be taught to dance. But only with careful planning and attention to the detailed change and embedding journey. It won't happen by putting the elephant in the ring and having the ringmaster wish for a pirouette.

Chris Mason is an innovation expert and founder of Triniti Marketing. www.trinitimarketing.com

How to Select the Best Ideas in the Innovation Funnel

Frank Mattes

The process of innovation is often represented by a funnel with a wide funnel opening—the fuzzy front-end that sucks in a huge number of ideas from within the company from suppliers or customers—and a strongly contoured funnel neck in which the selected and prepared projects are handled efficiently, or the efficient back-end. In practice, throughout the entire process, decision nodes or "gates" are installed, through which every idea and every project must pass. In these nodes, a defined, usually high-level gatekeeper team makes the decisions to go, kill or put on hold. How can innovation objects that have a deferment quality (vague ideas versus concrete concepts) be measured simultaneously, so that the firm can make solid decisions about where to invest its limited resources?

Naturally, innovative ideas in the fuzzy front-end of the innovation process are rather soft and can hardly be measured using hard valuation methods. Nevertheless, work on these ideas still requires time and budget resources. This is also the case for innovation work that refines rather concrete concepts, such as solving technical challenges.

There must be some sort of prioritization scheme in place to make sure that the most promising ideas get the innovation resources they need, and that innovation resources aren't fully spent just on tangible concepts. In other words, a firm needs to find an evaluation mechanism that allows for a simultaneous handling of fuzzy/soft ideas and solid/hard concepts.

Successful approaches for this mechanism build on scoring procedures. A cross-functional team evaluates some key dimensions by using, say, a scale that runs from 0 (unacceptable) to 5 (a perfect fit). Two points are important in applying these scoring mechanisms. First, if an idea scores below a minimum threshold at a Killer/Showstopper criterion, it must not be pursued further. Second, the applied criteria need to cover all relevant aspects of the innovation. Typically, these criteria include:

- Fit to innovation strategy
- Fit to the technology life cycle
- Fulfillment of success factors in the segment (technology, sales, supply chain)
- Intellectual Property situation
- Technical probability of success
- Achievable competitive position
- Size of the target market
- Expected discounted cash flow
- Expected margin

Using a process that builds on scoring mechanisms for ideas in the early, fuzzy front-end of the innovation funnel, firms get a consolidated view of all of their ideas and concepts. Then they can make profound decisions on how the resources should be split among, refining and testing vague ideas and refining concepts or solving technical challenges.

Frank Mattes works with catalyst innovation-3 and aims to help leading firms win in the third generation of innovation management, shaped by Open Collaborative Innovation and social networks.

Ad Astra Rocket 360°

Veronica Medina Orellana

For those who have met Dr. Franklin Chang Díaz, it is no surprise that Ad Astra is far from being just a company business—it's an absolutely innovative business microcosm.

Dr. Chang Díaz was the first naturalized US citizen to become a NASA astronaut, and is one of the men with the most missions and hours in space history. Ad Astra Rocket is a 360° business model because at the same time that the company is developing technology for global benefit, it is also providing local companies and young Costa Rican professionals a chance to participate in the global high technology market. This is key to understanding why it's 360°: a combination of business objective with the social scope of developing talent in Costa Rica. Dr. Chang Díaz wanted to make this remarkable contribution to our country.

A problem to solve, a business opportunity.
The large number of out of operation satellites orbiting the Earth began to pose a threat to future space missions, as well as other devices in operation. A clash between satellites from China and the United States in February 2009 alerted the UN and world's space agencies about the threat of space garbage. Over nearly five decades of space activities, 4,800 releases have put some 6,000 satellites into orbit; only about 800 remain in operation according to the European Space Agency (ESA). In addition to the large amount of intact space equipment, a total mass of 5,500 tons, there are many other objects orbiting the Earth. The Space Surveillance Network of the United States regularly monitors more than 12,000 of them.

Reducing travel costs for missions to clean up space was Dr. Chang Díaz's goal. He then came up with an innovation process that comprised a first stage of ideation (which actually started in 1973 with the study of behavior super hot gases called plasmas) and a second stage of engine prototyping (the plasma Variable Specific Impulse Magnetoplasma Rocket (VASIMR) at Massachusetts Institute of Technology in 1983), which led to a patent in 2002. This was followed by a third stage of developing a business model with the foundation of the first engine plasma factory in 2005 in Texas, and an affiliate company in Costa Rica. Finally, the fourth stage of innovation involves the prototype testing and development, which will be completed in 2011 and tested in 2012.

It's expected that this engine could halve the maintenance costs of the International Space Station. The actual cost is 240 million dollars per year; using the VASIMR, this value is expected to drop to 27 million dollars. In addition, the VASIMR hopes to reduce travel time to Mars from eight months to one.

The engine will also promote development of other business opportunities in the aerospace industry, such as space tourism. Currently, there's private investment in space travel with companies like SpaceX, Bigelow Aerospace, Scaled Composites and Virgin Galactic planning the development of subor-bital and orbital vehicles and modular space stations.

Ad Astra has established a partnership with different stakeholders in the space business, including NASA, which supported the project to make a space flight test in 2013. NASA's phased review process is considered a first-generation process in new product development—the Stage-Gate® model was suggested by Robert G. Cooper in 1986 and was further developed into the well-known Stage-Gate® Process. If we review the progression of VASIMR's development under the scope of the Stage-Gate® Process, we can organize the project actions in five doors of preparations to be addressed:

- Gate 1: Payload Integration Agreement signed in December 2009
- Gate 2: the Preliminary Design Review (PDR) planned for mid 2011
- Gate 3: Critical Design Review (CDR) in early 2012
- Gate 4: Certificate of Flight Readiness (CHEST) in mid 2013
- Gate 5: Flight Readiness Review in late 2013

The investment plan to develop the first VASIMR requires a total of 150 million dollars. The company partnership with NASA provides local and international investors with confidence in the project, and Ad Astra seeks mechanisms in the local financial market to aid in issuing shares and obtaining the resources needed for plasma engine development. After the first shares issuance, Ad Astra was the first company to use the figure of "limited public offering", which means that the titles can only be purchased by institutional investors. In 2011 Ad Astra is expected to make its Initial Public Offer (IPO) on the New York Stock Exchange. Once the IPO has been made, the company can complete its transition from a science project to a business technology project.

There are some important factors that made Ad Astra possible; the most important factor revolves around the persistence and systematic action of Dr. Chang Díaz. From an early age he dreamed of becoming an astronaut; his passion to follow this dream took him into space seven times, and led to the development of a global scientific solution that will save energy and let the world continue to enjoy the different services provided by existing satellites.

Veronica Medina Orellana *is Founder and President of New Product Creation, and works with the Product Development and Management Association of Central America. veronica@newproductcreation.com*

How Customers Can Restore Cracks in the Foundation of Businesses

Robert van Meer, Tim Meuleman

It's time to rethink the way we do business. A company's reason for existence and its relevance to customers are changing drastically. For a long time, knowing how to be efficient and relevant to consumers has been the core capability for any business. Thus, knowledge is the foundation of business. A shift is occurring, however. The networked society we now live in empowers customers. They can find each other easily online to share their ideas and combine their expertise. Wikileaks, for example, has shown that even the deepest political and business secrets cannot always be kept undisclosed.

Knowledge is no longer an exclusive asset or rare commodity—it's become common property. Many things are being solved these days with opensource solutions, involving groups of people connecting through the Internet. Wikipedia is the world's largest encyclopedia, created by the people. Open-farmtech.org delivers the 50 most important farming machine blueprints, making it simpler and cheaper to create tractors. The traditional manufacturer is being put out to pasture.

With knowledge as a commodity, a firm needs to possess more than knowledge in order to stay valuable for the consumer; they need *relevant* knowledge. Our belief is that companies can stay valuable in the long term if they restructure the fundamentals of their business into a new approach where three additional fundamentals are added.

Customer knowledge
The first capability lays the groundwork for the other two, involving customers. When customers get involved in business processes, the firm gains relevant knowledge that competitors cannot easily find. Customers know what they want and how they want it.

Customer involvement is also essential to value-creation. A firm no longer creates the value of its commodity by itself; value creation is a symbiotic process. A firm can offer a value proposition, but ultimately the consumer determines the real-world value of a product or service. As such, the value is determined through co-creation between a company and its customers. This perspective is called Service Dominant Logic. As customers are increasingly networked, empowered, and willing to participate, they can and will generate value without the interference of firms. We call this perspective Self-service Dominant Logic. It means that connecting with the consumer is essential to generating relevant value. By involving individuals and letting individuals co-create the value of the offering, the consumer will approach a company out of free will and be truly loyal. Not just individuals but entire market segments can be engaged in the long term, creating sustained company loyalty; something we call market loyalty.

Creativity
Unlike knowledge, creativity can be seen as everything new and as an inspiration that can result in relevant knowledge if adopted properly. It could be said that creativity is an alternative source of competence to knowledge. A creative firm has access to relevant knowledge; competitors do not.

There are more consumers willing to share their thoughts than employees to be hired. Using this immense source of human capital leads to an increase in creativity, resulting in out-of-the-box ideas and relevant innovation.

Value Facilitation
The real challenge is of course to assemble relevant knowledge, consumers, and creativity—and to stay efficient while doing so. Consumers will only participate in the value creation process if they are intrinsically motivated. One cannot force consumers to collaborate. The trick is to be skilled in process facilitation. One has to help consumers be value-creators. We call this last capability knowledge of how to facilitate value delivery.

YouTube is a good example of how these core competences can make a firm relevant. It acknowledges the fact that consumers have more collective access to video content than a traditional broadcaster does, so they use the consumers' desire to broadcast their own videos. Because millions of customers upload video content on a daily basis, the platform now possesses the biggest database of videos on demand in the world and has a competitive advantage to traditional broadcasters. Using the consumer helps YouTube stay efficient (no video production costs needed), to have access to more relevant knowledge (the biggest database of video content, namely consumers' conserved stock), and to enhance creativity (access to novel videos that haven't been broadcasted before). YouTube also facilitates the process of building an environment where consumers who want to share and consumers who want to consume come together.

The future of business is two worlds becoming one; firms should no longer merely be delivering value to consumers (B2C) or other firms (B2B), and the empowered consumer is able and willing to create value for companies. They will share brilliance and spark innovation, and firms will embrace this change. A new marketplace has arisen, a market bursting with new opportunities and a new playground for the new leaders: the C2B market place.

Robert van Meer and Tim Meuleman are authors of The C2B Revolution *and managing partners of C2B consultancy.*

Case Study of the Phase Between Idea Generation and Launch

Cock Meerhof

Innovation delivery is an important part of innovation realization; we learned to appreciate this during a recent innovation process. Radical innovation has been taken seriously at Univé for the past four years. The usual paths we took concerning product development—in this case regarding insurance policies—were discarded and new business sought, found and developed. Innovation is only true when a new, creative idea actually gets to market. But innovation in a company with risk avoidance in its genes demands a process that provides a level of certainty and reassurance. During the idea generation phase, Univé used the FORTH method—a good, streamlined process with an almost guaranteed result. But then came the next phase...

As internal innovation consultant, I developed and implemented a new mobility concept. After extensive research into possible alternatives, a business case was developed that was accepted by both the director and commissioning party. I then had to make the concept market ready, but Univé needed partners to do this. This required co-creation.

Each step of the innovation process, from idea generation to implementation, demands a different skill. Where conceptual thinkers are needed for the generation phase, entrepreneurs are essential in implementation. We called on pro-Actuate consultants, die-hard experts in innovation delivery, to help us with our implementation stage. We followed their Innovation Flywheel model as a guideline for our approach, experimenting and developing using short, fast revolutions that made implementation faster and better. Thanks to the tight deadline we set ourselves, not to mention our enthusiasm and the speed with which we worked, we gained the confidence of both our internal and external contacts.

Some of the lessons we learned during our innovation delivery process can be summarized in the following tips:

- Keep the concept or idea compact and retain ideas for expansion for later. For instance, we restricted ourselves to the private market, although opportunities were also seen for the b2b market.

- Keep flexible and seize opportunities. Although our target group initially comprised the 50-plussers, the youth market also showed potential.

- Be bold and stay ahead of decisions. Even before we had the official go-ahead, we had an order on the books.

- If you work with external partners, ensure they apply their expertise and not their standard processes. This should form one of the selection criteria for partner choice as otherwise your solution will be sub-optimal in terms of price and/or process.

- A pilot phase can work for and against you. Although a pilot phase may get the go-ahead more quickly from a decision-maker (and you get to learn from the experience), it can also be halted just as quickly. In this case, every advantage has its disadvantage.

- Ensure the line organization is kept directly involved or part responsible. We had the full support of the directors, but the line managers needed to keep being drawn in. Ideally everyone should have the same drive to make the product a success.

- Create concrete and flexible goals for test or pilot phases. Don't just look at the sales and test results of the process, but also consider image, contribution to brand stretching and the like.

- Bear in mind that if you seem to have an advantage and are unique in the market, that this is a temporary advantage. There are now comparable products to our innovation already on the market. If you want to benefit from first-mover advantage, you have to push ahead, pick up the pace, and follow your instinct by going against the grain.

In short, delivery is vital to a successful innovation, and a good process such as the Innovation Flywheel model will prove its worth.

Cock Meerhof is senior manager Innovation at Univé-VGZ-IZA-Trias

Better Delivery of New Innovation By Doing Three Things at Once

David Midgley

There are many reasons why great ideas that emerge from the front-end of innovation don't get effective delivery at the back-end. There's the difficulty of translating concepts and business cases into working products or services, the many technical hurdles that must be overcome to get the innovation on the market and the difficulty of persuading customers to change from the status quo. However, in my experience the main reason is simple: organizational people. Organizations, especially large ones, have many creative ways to prevent innovation from happening. This is particularly true for major innovation, which will be my focus.

Some of these barriers to innovation are due to conflict of interest—the old business refuses to make way for the new—but many are due to a failure to understand the requirements and implications of major innovation. These problems have existed for a long time and are well documented, starting with Machiavelli several centuries ago. However, they've taken on a new urgency in the last decade as the nature of innovation has itself changed. Innovation is less about new products and more about new services, value chains and business models. In other words, innovation is more about new ways of orchestrating the effective delivery of benefits to the customer. Think about Apple with the App Store, Zara with fast fashion or IBM as a consulting firm.

For many large multinationals, the speed of this change in thinking about innovation is hard to digest. Many are still in a new product mindset—with limited services, traditional distribution channel structures and mainstream management practices. For example, large organizations with internal silos find it hard to deliver integrated solutions to customers. Yet increasingly this is what customers—particularly B2B customers—want. Also, many managers struggle with Web 2.0 and the challenge of Generation Z consumers yet these consumers will have all the spending power in less than a decade. All large organizations find it hard to evolve and mutate their organizational structures to introduce new business models in a smooth and successful manner.

To me the way out of these problems lies in:

- Harnessing the power of diversity and networks in innovation teams

- Developing organizational capabilities for continuous change

- Learning to work with partner organizations

None of these should come as surprise; they've been on the agenda for several years, but few organizations are able to do all three at once.

Harnessing the diversity of different mindsets and experiences by carefully choosing and preparing the team is crucial. That provides the basis for breaking out of the existing industry or firm mentality. The team should include people who are well connected with the power structure of the rest of the organization, and capable of working within that structure to effect change. Innovation teams are as much change agents as idea creators.

Those requirements can be supplemented by change management skills, and senior leaders need to think more about change as continuous rather than episodic. What rules and incentives will best support and encourage continuous innovation in the organization structure and business model? As major innovation often includes the value chain, both leaders and teams need skills in working with partner organizations to assemble the right capabilities and resources to deliver innovation. Better innovation delivery is all about capabilities and organization—all about people.

David Midgley is Professor of Marketing at INSEAD. www.theinnovationmanual.com, www.insead.edu

How a Toothbrush Made WD-40 a Better Product

Graham Milner

The WD-40 multi-purpose product has changed very little over 40 years. Our loyal end users have taken the brand into about 85% of US homes and over 170 countries worldwide. For decades, there seemed to be very little meaningful innovation that could be brought to the "blue and yellow can with the red straw".

We were however, quite aware of one consistent complaint: "I always lose the straw!"

We looked at many improvements—devices that attach the straw to the side of the can were the most common. But all of them increased the cost of the can. As a brand, WD-40 has always been committed to exceeding end user expectations at extremely good value. So an extra penny or two or five to replace the sticky tape that held the straw to the can just didn't seem like a good decision.

One day Gad Shaanan of Gad Shaanan Design came to see me on a pitch visit. Gad retold the tale of the toothbrush; an item that for years had seen innovation as cheaper and cheaper brushes until the commoditized market had settled in at a 99-cent price point. Then along came Johnson and Johnson and the Reach toothbrush, a roughly four-dollar item .By adding real end-user value, it was a major hit. This was followed by increasingly more sophisticated innovation that now results in everything from 99-cent toothbrushes to 500-dollar electric wonders. The Reach innovation broke the paradigm. (In the interest of full disclosure, my telling of this story may not be 100% factually accurate. Neither Gad nor I are experts in the oral care category. It doesn't change the basic insight that drove this innovation.

That got me thinking, and we contracted Gad Shaanan to design a solution to our lost straw dilemma. Five years later, and with literally millions of dollars in cumulative incremental sales, the WD-40 Smart Straw has driven growth in the apparently tapped out United States, as well as many other countries. It continues to be a brand growth engine, with increasing global penetration.

So a consumer complaint and a lesson from a completely unrelated category combined to make the second biggest innovation in our company's history. The first was, of course, the persistence of a chemist who after 39 tries finally gave us Water Displacement Formula Number 40—WD-40. A few lessons learned:

- Consumer complaints are a rich source of innovation ideas

- Cost and value are different, and we need to challenge ourselves when we confuse them in innovation

- An outside perspective is very valuable

Sometimes you need that fresh perspective to see what you're missing!

Graham Milner works with WD-40. www.wd40.com

Entrepreneurial Lenses
on the Three *D*s

Mark B. Mondry

Entrepreneurship, or intrapreneurship in large organizations, is driven by the thrill and excitement of creating something new. When something new is created we deem ourselves innovative—a label currently cherished by every company, large and small. Yet as we all know, newness itself is never enough to make something commercially successful. Many entrepreneurs have been intoxicated by the pure newness/innovativeness of their idea or technology, only to fail spectacularly in the pursuit of bringing it to market.

The innovation process itself plays the critical role in achieving commercial success, and successful entrepreneurs respect this. Beginning with the identification of a worthy opportunity to pursue in the first place, the innovation process includes morphing the opportunity into an actual new product or service and making it available and valuable to both actual and potential customers. Each phase takes on new meaning in the entrepreneurial context.

Although there are numerous models available to define the innovation process, let us utilize a simple one known as the Three *D*'s. The Three *D*'s define a three-phase process: Discovery, Development, and Delivery. Although these phases are generally sequential, and in some cases circular, not all of the three phases are equally challenging.

Discovery
There's been extensive research and practical focus on the first phase of the innovation process, Discovery. This phase is about identifying the appropriate opportunity to pursue, the essence of entrepreneurship. It's well established that this first phase has tremendous impact on the likelihood of commercial success. Basically, pull-innovation is far more successful than push-innovation. New products and services that respond to real customer problems, needs, wants or desires are far more likely to be commercially successful then products or services based on fancy technologies in search of a way to make money. Many refined tools and approaches are available for the Discovery phase, though the iterative and collaborative process makes the picture a bit fuzzy from the entrepreneurial perspective. Hence

the well accepted nomenclature "fuzzy front-end." This phase can be challenging to entrepreneurs who see things only through their own lens.

Development
The Development phase of the innovation process moves from fuzzy to focused. This phase involves engineering, design, material selection, prototyping, testing, validation and other disciplines that are clarify, simplify and transform fuzzy concepts produced in the Discovery phase into concrete tangible products and services. For the entrepreneur this phase is about gaining clarity, comparing available alternatives and making choices. Because many specific technical tasks in this phase can be collaboratively outsourced to specialists in other organizations, a typical entrepreneur erroneously views this phase as a mere technical process to be expedited in the urgency to get to market.

Delivery
Now the fog sets in, and things become fuzzy again. I believe the Delivery phase has evolved to become the most differentiating phase in commercial success. Delivery is not just about making the new offering physically accessible to customers; it is about doing so artfully through an alluring, enthralling value proposition that's enthusiastically embraced by potential customers. This includes crafting a brand experience around your offering that speaks to emotional and lifestyle desires, ultimately creating a product or service that customers want to be associated with.

This phase should build from the Discovery gained in the first phase. Commercial success isn't about your technology; it's about facilitating a positive user experience throughout the product lifecycle from initial exposure to ultimate retirement or disposal. This includes packaging, advertising, support, product image, sustainability, and the dynamics of the user community you build. That's why Apple's iPhone and iPad are more successful than the numerous smart phone and tablet alternatives available.

Many entrepreneurs fail to visualize Discovery and Delivery in a combined lens. Rather, they see Development and Delivery as part of the same race to get an offering to market. The elements of a successful offering can be unclear and dynamic. Welcome to the "blurry back-end" of innovation.

Mark B. Mondry, *NPDP, CLP, is Managing Director at Phronesys, LLC. www.phronesys.com*

Managing Successful Innovation Delivery

Desai Narasimhalu

If we define innovation delivery as the actual execution and implementation of an innovation, then we can identify three main reasons why it fails: emotional attachment to initial ideas, lack of project management experience and absence of cross-functional teams.

Emotional attachment
Many entrepreneurs start pushing a technology innovation without understanding the market demand for it. These creators of technologies firmly believe in their technologies' apparent worth, and generally do not pay much heed to market feedback. However, innovations have been delivered successfully to the market when the innovators were ready to adapt or even abandon their initial ideas after receiving feedback. Innovators should use a rapid prototyping approach to sense and respond to market needs. The market will accept innovations that address a need with open arms. However, innovations that just provide a solution that's "good to have" are usually met with initial resistance. Therefore, innovators should ensure that they are indeed pursuing innovations that address a "must have" need rather than a "good to have" want.

Project management
Some innovators don't have project management experience that is essential to successful innovation delivery. It would be useful if all innovators who were involved in innovation delivery had training in general project management principles and iterative innovation development methodologies. The latter would focus on first delivering the key features of an innovation that selected target customers consider most relevant. Such training should include identifying risks and developing mitigation plans for handling those risks. There are generally at least three types of key risks:

- When a critical resource from the founding team walks away. There should be a contingency plan for a replacement should this happen.

- When the innovation faces an unexpected adoption hurdle in the target market. Contingency plans for an agile redesign and development process ought to be already thought through in the innovation development methodology.

- When competitors appear on the horizon. Again, it is important to have plans for tackling competition, whether they involve dropping prices or offering new value.

Cross-functional teams

The absence of cross-functional teams is a critical issue that will have a major impact on the success of an innovation delivery. A well-balanced team that has members with significant experience in topics such as technology, marketing/sales, usability and experience design and channel management will understand the market needs and design and deliver innovations accordingly. When a team isn't internally balanced, it can still achieve balance by either outsourcing the relevant functions to experts or finding partners with expertise.

Managing successful innovation delivery therefore translates into creating a well-balanced team that is well versed in rapid and iterative innovation development using robust project management techniques and can sense and respond to market feedback.

Desai Narasimhalu, Singapore Management University.

EUREKA: Support for Innovation and Entrepreneurship

Niki Naska

Since its launch in 1985, the intergovernmental EUREKA network continues to be highly effective in mobilizing Europe's capability to innovate. For the past 26 years this decentralized network has enabled small- and medium-sized companies (SMEs), larger industries, research centers, universities and national administrations to join forces in realizing near-market research and development and innovation (R&D&I) through transnational collaborative projects. The results can be seen in a dramatic transformation of key industry sectors—and in hundreds of new products, materials and processes that add significantly to the quality of our daily lives.

The unprecedented success of Eurostars, a joint initiative co-funded by EUREKA member countries and the European Union, is particularly noteworthy. In the two-year life span of the initiative, more than 720 SMEs led agreements for market-driven project generation. An average of 67% of Eurostars participants have been R&D-performing SMEs.

The crystallographer Hubert Curien—a former president of the European Space Agency and father of the Ariane rocket—in his capacity as French Research Minister convinced both François Mitterand and Helmut Kohl to create EUREKA in 1985. This great visionary's support continued until his death in 2005. In an interview, Professor Curien discussed the motivation behind the creation of EUREKA and whether its ambitions had been realized. He explained;

> "The idea for EUREKA came when Ronald Reagan was launching his Strategic Defense Initiative—popularly known as Star Wars. The SDI had a military objective, but it was clear that such huge expenditure would also stimulate development of the most advanced technology. Europe did not want a military program, preferring a civilian initiative giving technology a kick-start. We wanted to promote a bottom-up approach.

We did not want to decree at government level what would be good for industry and research, but to listen to the proposals of researchers and industrialists to set up innovative projects that would also have a unifying effect. Bureaucracy had to be avoided. We did not want to define sectors in advance. We could easily have drawn up a list that included optronics, advanced electronics and information technology. It was obvious that these areas would benefit from the SDI. But we did not want to put any constraints on imagination. The field was open to ideas of all kinds. Clearly, achieving technological parity with the United States was one idea. What is important is to live in a balanced world. This cannot be so if a single nation, however important, can claim technological monopolies in vital areas. We have seen this in the space sector, where Europe must have an independent means of getting into space. Early partners were the most wealthy and technologically advanced nations. Newer countries don't have the same capacity. But we nevertheless wanted to welcome them to EUREKA so this initiative could be a unifying factor between all the countries of Europe, and in particular Eastern Europe. This hasn't brought in any substantial resources but has reinforced the idea of European cohesion. The overall assessment of EUREKA is positive. We've worked hard. I believe EUREKA has played a very positive role in bringing public laboratories and industry together. Public laboratories saw an opportunity to access additional funding—something they couldn't ignore— and to work on ideas that would have an opportunity to be developed. The technological panorama has changed considerably over the years, in particular with the emergence of life sciences. I don't think EUREKA has run out of steam. We need to continue to sustain it. We should not believe that this program will last forever, but EUREKA has not exhausted its potential."

Niki Naska works with EUREKA.

Where Has All the 8-Dimensional Imagination Gone?

Kobus Neethling

It's obvious to me that most of the hundreds of from the "idea to innovation" models are, to a large degree, remakes of one another. Remaking, probing and searching are how the mind seeks uniqueness. Unfortunately, uniqueness seems much more prevalent in the ideation stage than in the delivery stage. Since 1950 Creativity and innovation experts have focused extensively on creating, developing, assessing and improving ideas. There's been far less commitment and passion towards breakthrough delivery methods and practices. Maybe the biggest mistake is to still believe that there should be total separation between the imaginer and the practitioner; that delivering means step by step and that there's no space for the intuitive "AHA!" during implementation. The one overriding issue in all of this is that idea creation has always been as much heart as mind. But for the past 50 years idea delivery has been dominated by the mind. In the 21st Century, however, innovation delivery without passion and imagination has very little chance of changing the antiquated status quo.

With more than two decades as a Torrance scholar, creativity and innovation researcher, trainer, author of more than 80 books, creator and implementer of new ideas under my belt, I've been exposed to hundreds of creativity and innovation models. The most spectacular innovation that I have ever witnessed and, in some small way, been part of is the creation of a new South Africa. In a television series that I co-wrote with Sid Parnes, one of my mentors and one of the great pioneers of creative problemsolving, was called *Creating a Miracle*. In the series we unpacked the process from the pre-idea stage to the formation stage. The essence of this process could be summed up as follows:

- The insight and understanding that a new dispensation (innovation) was necessary. Initially only by the majority and not by the decision makers

- Persuading opponents to the innovation to accept the inescapability of change

- Forming the initial idea team representing all stakeholders (the 'filling of every chair' philosophy), not only to create the strategies and formulate a joint vision but to also identify possible stumbling blocks and eliminate them before they happen

- Selecting and empowering new teams to

    - Research and analyze ideas
    - Address fears and resistance
    - Create acceptance
    - Formulate implementation strategies and details

- Actualizing big picture ideas like changing the composition of government and changing the national anthem and flag,

- Actualizing the ideas (phases 1-10)

These last phases have proved to be the most difficult to make happen—as is the case with most business and product innovations. The reasons have been documented over and over again—lack of synergy between the strategists and implementers, too little focus on environment and culture preparation, lack of specific implementation skills, far less excitement about the final outcomes than the creation of newness and lack of passion at certain phases of the delivery process.

Kobus Neethling is President of the South African Creativity Foundation.

Connect, Cooperate and Share

Jos Nelissen

We all know the scientist Thomas Edison invented the light bulb. What you probably don't know is that at least 10 other scientists also invented the light bulb—some of them even earlier than Edison.

Why did we forget all these names? Probably because Edison was the only scientist who had the idea of developing complementary instruments like the dynamo, cables, safety fuses, socket, and a meter for power consumption. He also started a trial in a small village so as to ensure that the product worked in practice, and he filed some patents.

Thomas Edison made this invention successful because, while being a researcher, he thought as a businessman; that is, from the consumer perspective. That's exactly what we do in my company Newtricious, in the development of *nutraceuticals*—food-based products that help to regain or maintain health.

We begin with a quick search for new ideas and we try to answer initial questions: Is there a consumer need (is there a market, how big is it, is it growing, can it be reached)? Are there any competitors? What's necessary in research & development? Which partners do we need in order to build a strong and complete consortium that can develop a successful innovation and market introduction?

Then comes one of the main challenges for successful innovation delivery: creating a consortium that covers the total chain, from researchers to market experts, but most importantly the consumer. Bringing market experts and patent specialists together in research project teams helps us to not only work on products with health claims (for example, that it prevents a disease), but to also successfully bring these innovations to the consumer. Innovation delivery doesn't start when the product is ready; it starts at the very first idea, before the fundamental research is even designed.

Working in multidisciplinary teams is fun. There's a lot of cross-fertilization, and the researcher not only gets questions concerning his specialty but also if what he's working on is in the consumer's interest. The researcher and the patent specialist ask the marketer how he intends to position a product, and together they design the R&D program. This multidimensional approach is truly inspiring, and good for progress as it stimulates creativity—the team gets lots of new ideas to work on.

All partners report to the project team on a regular basis, and Newtricious feels privileged to manage this process that goes beyond normal business management. Innovation management is about openness, flexibility and the ability to handle and react on results—especially if they are sometimes unexpected. In this process we try to build a climate where, from a business perspective, the focus is on our mission to develop products that help people improve their quality of life.

Throughout this process we keep Edison in mind; for over one hundred and thirty years, his invention and the successful development of the light bulb has improved the quality of our lives. This great innovation—its business approach and the attention paid to all aspects of the development and market positioning—is exemplary. We continue to work in cooperation with partners by connecting and sharing on small and large innovations that can really make a difference to society.

Jos Nelissen is an entrepreneur in Agro, Food & Life Sciences.

Entrepreneurs, Innovation Leadership and Blind Driving

Victor Newman

Understanding innovation leadership is a bit like driving a car. Currently, most organizations manage their psychology of innovation like blind drivers. It's possible to become relatively successful at leading an organization through the medium of traditional performance measures, which are much like the cues a blind driver would use to stay in the correct lane on the motorway. By hearing the irregular sound cues of tires bumping over reflective cat's eyes marking traffic lanes on one side of the car, and a screeching noise on the side of oncoming traffic, a crude form of progress can be managed—even if getting onto and off the motorway is frightening. It clearly can be done, but is it a sustainable approach?

The key to successful leadership of innovation begins with understanding:

- The four Innovation Leadership Behaviors (ILB)

- The limitations of where you are now in terms of your actual ILB profile and the nature of the challenge in terms of your preferred ILB profile

- How hungry you are for change, and how much you want to take control and do something about it

For some leaders, the idea of developing an understanding of their own ILB profiles (actual and preferred) can be intimidating, much as primitive tribes were afraid that photography would steal their souls. They act as if the study and search to understand behavioral patterns would destroy the power of a secret formula by exposing it. But as they say at the Royal Air Force's Parachute Training School, knowledge dispels fear. This knowledge is essential—once you have it, it becomes possible to ask yourself: What can I contribute to making this organization more successful? What kind of innovation leadership should I be working on? And how can I develop myself to make a difference and become more effective?

The Four Innovation Leadership Behaviors (ILBs)
For innovation to occur in an organization, you need a mix of at least four generic types of Innovating Leadership Behaviors: Creators, Translators, Stabilizers and Navigators. When planned for, encouraged and balanced correctly, they can promote and deliver continuous innovation.

- Creators provide the source of new, disruptive ideas

- Stabilizers build quality delivery systems for products and services

- Translators connect new ideas to new opportunities

- Navigators anticipate what's coming, know when to get in and when to get out, and how to manage it.

In essence, the ILB model suggests that the 2 definitive dimensions involved are Discipline and Contextual Awareness. Discipline is the conscious application of something to get work done, and Contextual Awareness is the conscious, interpretive behavior within the context of a continuously evolving market context, where tomorrow's work and value is nothing like today's. The generalizations made through the ILB model reflect both the limitations and the power of working with stereotypes.

In this situation:

- The Navigator is both highly disciplined and has high contextual awareness in the form of helicopter thinking (the ability to move flexibly from a tactical to a strategic perspective, and back again), with the ability to see the bigger picture outside the constraints of the local situation or market, and can consciously apply mental models to interpret the health of the organization or its strategy.

- The Translator has low discipline but high contextual awareness; he or she pays lip service to the dominant form of work-discipline associated with managing the performance of current products, services and processes (due to being aware that the status quo is obviously decaying, which creates a vacuum that needs to be filled with something else).

- The Creator tends towards a low discipline threshold with a relatively low contextual awareness because he or she is intrinsically motivated by intellectual ideas and patterns outside the dominant business context, which tends towards reinforcing existing forms of business value. Creators respond to their own intellectual vision and have an autonomous ability to see patterns and gaps in current ideas.

- The Stabilizer tends towards inflexibility, with high levels of conscious discipline to define work (Stabilizers love disciplined work ideologies) but have a low contextual awareness (which can mean the application of a discipline beyond its usefulness or sell-by date). He or she tends not to notice the growing need to move into a new discipline, to move into a new technology or new market, instead taking as a given that the existing work environment is not negotiable.

Victor Newman is Visiting Professor at the University of Greenwich and CIO of Milamber Group.

Innovation in Social Enterprise

Tim Nicol

Enterprise is getting social, but can the principles and practices of innovation management be applied to the "third sector?" Absolutely. There's a transformation going on in the UK in which the "third sector"—that part of the economy that lies between the public and private sectors—is growing both in size and importance. If it's not of professional interest to you, chances are you have some personal interest in a third sector organization as a user, donor, governor, or other stakeholder. Social enterprises characterize the third sector, i.e. businesses whose three bottom lines are financial, social, and environmental. As such, there are always tradeoffs and conflicts to manage, just like in a private sector business. So what's new?

I've spent the last 18 months planning and managing a startup social enterprise in an English village as part of the BBC/BIG Lottery Fund "Village SOS" program. This experiment, televised on BBC One in the summer of 2011, was designed to examine if enterprises can inspire a village life revival in the UK, with all the social benefits that it brings, and be sustained by a functioning business that generates its own revenues after a pump-priming capital grant.

I've helped to establish "Taste Tideswell," a project aiming to boost the local economy of Tideswell in the Peak District by driving the local food economy and educating people in every aspect of the local food chain. Taste Tideswell Ltd. built and operates a cookery school and teaching microbrewery, with conference facilities and a commercial kitchen plus a brand license scheme to support startup business.

Before this personal sudden rush of social conscience, I ran my own innovation consultancy and worked for an FMCG multinational across many European markets with a focus on branded innovation and NPD activity. Did that experience come in handy for my baptism into the third sector? Yes indeed.

Social Enterprises are now obliged to become more commercial in order to survive with reduced grant funding, and the people that run them are becoming more business oriented—many are migrants from the private sector anyway. Social Enterprises are taking on the responsibility of running large chunks of the economy and helping people to help themselves. Market forces and the needs of service users/customers increasingly drive the business models, not central government spending. So the principles and practices of management, marketing, and innovation are all tools of the trade, whichever bottom line you are aiming to improve.

My background in branded marketing and innovation has come in handy in Tideswell. We've run the project in a businesslike way right from the start, and planning and managing it as a business instead of a cause or campaign. We start with the consumer/ stakeholders, looking at their needs and wants and searching for unsatisfied demand and insights. Ideas and plans were developed and screened against the kind of criteria we use in front-end innovations screening, including capability, strategy, and demand.

The shape of the business—a complex, multifaceted one, covering as many touch points as possible on the local food chain—was molded into a cohesive strategy with a clear mission and synergy built in throughout. For example, we want to save our local food retailers from extinction. How does a cookery school do that? By teaching local people more about the origins of their food and how to prepare it, we think they'll want to buy more basic ingredients—which is what local artisan shops and producers tend to make and sell.

Having developed the concept and the business plan, we got into execution mode. Delivery on a tight timescale and budget was critical not just to get the revenue in as soon as possible, but also to beat the clock of a 12-month deadline for the lottery funding and TV coverage. We developed brand positioning statements and design executions with the help of brand strategy and design experts, ("Peter and Paul", Sheffield's finest agency), and applied clear and consistent branding online, on paper, and on the building. We designed products (cookery courses) according to needs and wants, not what we thought was easy or good for people. Healthy eating cookery courses don't sell; Chocolate, Cupcakes, and Curry (and Brewing) *do*. Now that we're selling, we get constant feedback and continually refresh or replace courses in the portfolio. We're running at 95% overall satisfaction; as I write, we're testing a new jam making course downstairs in the kitchen.

We're a business so we use business techniques, and they work. Our aim is to achieve financial sustainability soon and break even on a monthly basis, so we can reinvest any surplus in our social obligations to the community: teaching local children and their parents about growing, cooking, making, and selling good food.

Tim Nicol is owner of MIH-Make Innovation Happen and Village Champion for Taste Tideswell, part of the BBC/BIG Lottery program "Village SOS." www.mihcentre.co.uk , www.tastetideswell.co.uk

Delivery Through an Open Innovation Approach

Sarah Pearson

Open Innovation, essentially the process of looking outside traditional company boundaries for ideas, is used to accelerate the innovation process and provide access to new technology and products the company wouldn't have dreamed of on its own. The usual focus when initiating an open innovation approach is accessing as many diverse ideas as possible. Successful approaches tend to be more strategic; they start by understanding what the company's searching for, how and where to look, what sort of negotiation strategies to use, and how to then manage any collaborations. But if the approach ends there, the crucial importance of market delivery gets missed. Many ideas end up shelved before they get a chance to bring value to the company because market delivery wasn't paid attention to. The strategies that can be used to overcome this include keeping delivery in mind from the start, targeted communication, and the importance of both internal and external networks.

When we set up Open Innovation at Cadbury, we knew we needed support from both the R&D and the Marketing teams right from the start. R&D teams had to tell us about the technical challenges they wanted assistance with in the product development phase; their involvement would be crucial for technology de-risking in the development phases of new technology. The Marketing teams made final decisions regarding launch plans, and understood long-term consumer insights. Gaining their support ensured that we could align breakthrough products with knowledge of broad consumer needs, and by working with them to understand the commercial possibilities.

The biggest challenge to this multidisciplinary approach is cultural. At Cadbury, we utilized targeted communication to overcome the barrier by developing concept designs and template opportunity descriptions. Concept drawings that showed what the new product could look like, alongside detailed descriptions of commercial opportunities, were used to communicate with both the R&D and Marketing teams. We developed these with their input, so the templates contained technical and commercial information that facilitated the decision process.

Constant communication was required to maintain the momentum, and technological opportunities were updated as new applications came to light. We kept in constant communication with both teams to make sure our search list remained up to date; as an added bonus, they took ownership of our search list.

Using this approach, we developed strong internal networks with a number of internal functions, including R&D, Marketing, Legal and Manufacturing. We balanced this with strong external networks that we used for new technology and product searches. External networks weren't just a source of ideas; they were also useful for concept design and product prototype development. We found that once R&D and Marketing teams had bought into the concept, they still needed tactile, physical prototypes before making a final decision. On various occasions we used external partners, with their new technology and process expertise, to help develop these prototypes. This external approach helped us access skills that weren't within the company and allowed us to develop prototypes faster through leveraging our external resources.

Utilizing these strategies, the team set up roughly 35 collaborations between Cadbury and external partners over an 18-month period. Some of these led to new product development, and a few managed to reduce time to market for planned product launches. Additionally, the development of an open culture led to 50% of long-term research projects involving external partners. Open Innovation became an integral part of the global innovation strategy, involving numerous functions in the planning phase.

Sarah Pearson is the Director of ANU Edge and a Visiting Fellow of the College of Business and Economics, The Australian National University. www.anuedge.anu.edu.au

Use Co-Creation to Put Innovation on a Fast Track to Success

Cheryl Perkins

Innovation is adapting to a new age. Companies deal with many more challenges today than in the past, and have to compete harder than ever to create and communicate new products and services. They're seeking ways to quickly discover and implement new ideas; many are turning to the power of co-creation.

Co-creation is an increasingly popular innovation trend in which companies ask customers, partners and other communities or networks for help with innovating their business models to create new sources of value—and it's making a big impact on the way companies are bringing new products or product enhancements to market. Many companies find that collaborative partnerships can lead to new opportunities for innovative products and services, and even yield entirely new market areas. They're also discovering how online communities can solve some of their toughest innovation problems, as well as how to build their business around an existing crowd of passionate people.

We learned about the importance of co-creation first-hand in November 2010, when my team completed our bi-annual survey of some of the leading companies driving global innovation. In the survey, respondents were asked to rank their top sources for innovative ideas—and placed employees and customers at the top of the list.

Many companies in a wide array of industries use collaboration to ideate, test and introduce products to the marketplace. Kraft Foods explored customer collaboration with the launch of the Innovatewithkraft.com website, where anyone can submit ideas for new products, processes or advertising. Here internal employees can set up idea competitions and utilize tools for quickly harvesting products that are "market-ready."

Previously Kraft offered an open phone line to its customers, who could call with questions, complaints, or ideas for new products or improvements. The company's site was the very first attempt at breaking out of its internal focus for gathering innovative ideas. Since the site launched, open innovation has brought many recent packaging enhancements to market, including the Oreo Snack 'n' Seal package, the Maxwell House Flavor Lock Lid and composite canister, and the package for Trident Xtra Care gum with Recaldent.

Similarly, Procter & Gamble has leveraged the idea of "collective intelligence" through their Connect and Develop program. One of their approaches is to link thousands of their researchers, developers and engineers with external innovators via blogs and wikis. The effort isn't just an exercise to see what might happen, but has a measurable corporate goal of 50% external innovation.

Whether you're a large consumer products company or a small startup, forming new connections with customers, employees, users or community groups can be a key strategy in the successful delivery of breakthrough innovations that stick. Focus on adaptability, an increased time-to-market and technology in order to keep up with the changing environment around you, and win the battle against the competition.

Cheryl Perkins is President and Founder of Innovationedge. www.innovationedge.com

Deep Consumer Insights:
The Key to Successful Delivery

Roger Peverelli, Reggy de Feniks

In financial services, most ideas traditionally originate from what is technically possible. With the power shifting to consumers, outside-in is the inevitable model of the future. Financial services companies will have to show improvements in understanding consumers. Their chances of successincrease dramatically when their new ideas are built on deep consumer insight.

A consumer insight is discovering something true about consumers that a company can use to really connect with their lives. This discovery is deliberate, since finding such an insight goes much further than typical consumer research. Consumer insights are rooted in consumer trends. In our book *Reinventing Financial Services: What Consumers Expect from Future Banks and Insurers*, we identified key consumer trends that set the stage for future innovation. By tapping into these trends, innovation can hit just the right consumer note.

Consumers are calling for transparency and simplicity
Transparency is the single most important factor in corporate reputation; there's a call for simplicity driven by choice and information overload. Our experience indicates that this goes beyond just products and also requires major adaptations to business models. However, differentiation is more difficult when all products are transparent and simple, so there should be a shift in the focus of innovation towards creating simple experiences; services and customer journeys that are simple, engaging and distinctive.

Consumers rely on the wisdom of crowds
People prefer the unbiased opinions of their fellow citizens and consumers in social media to a beautifully wrapped corporate message, and social media is perfectly suited for co-creating, piloting, testing and learning. But the innovation challenge is leveraging the wisdom of crowds as an integral part of the offering, for example by allowing peer-to-peer comparison and support.

Consumers are revaluing values

Consumers worldwide long for institutions that care, more than ever before. In essence, "ethics" is about doing honest, open and fair business. Recommend only those products you would buy yourself. Treat customers the way you would like to be treated as soon as you change your company outfit for consumer clothes, and you'll find new points of departure for innovation.

There are three other trends that are specifically important for the financial sector:

- Consumers' relationship with financial institutions has changed

- Consumers become more and more self-directed

- Consumers prefer to feel close

Roger Peverelli is a Partner at strategy and innovation consultancy VODW.
Reggy de Feniks is a Partner at strategy consultancy 9senses. This article is an extract from an earlier article from their book Reinventing Financial Services: What Consumers Expect from Future Banks and Insurers. *www.reinventingfinancialservices.com.*

Innovation Fault Lines

Jeffrey Phillips

In geological terms, a fault line is where two tectonic plates meet. People who live along fault lines, in California for example, often feel the effects of the fault lines when the plates slip, causing earthquakes or tremors. Occasionally these fault lines are visible, when the ground opens up to expose chasms. Some faults, however, are inactive and often exist without producing any evidence of their existence.

Like Earth, businesses have fault lines. Some of those fault lines lie well beneath the surface, and others are exposed. But unlike geographic fault lines, these faults don't cause monumental shifts. Business faults often act to prevent disruptive ideas and concepts from advancing. To innovate successfully, a firm must identify these fault lines and understand the barriers they present. Ideas often encounter business fault lines; when they do, they never change for the better. Here are four business fault lines, or chasms, that become barriers to innovation delivery:

Clear Strategy
No matter how dedicated innovators are to their ideas, if those solutions aren't aligned to corporate strategy they'll be rejected. There are two possible failures: either corporate strategy hasn't been clearly defined or it hasn't been effectively communicated. Either way, if the strategy is misunderstood or absent innovators will define ideas according to their own interpretations of needs and scope, which frequently don't match corporate goals. This makes innovation appear frivolous, since the ideas aren't addressing corporate strategies and needs.

Important, relevant customer need
All too often firms create new products and services based on what they *think* the customer wants or needs, rather than spending time finding out what the customer *actually* wants and needs. Firms that fail to spot trends or interact with customers and prospects can create interesting ideas that have no customer value or don't meet important customer objectives. Valuable, unarticulated needs are only discovered through careful research.

Transition from concept to product or services

Perhaps the largest chasm in an innovation effort is the transition of a well-conceived idea from an "innovation" activity to a new product or service development. While the innovation seems important and valuable, priorities, objectives and funding for development teams are set years in advance. It's difficult for even a very compelling idea to cross the chasm and become a prioritized project for the product or service development team. This chasm causes many good ideas to fail due to lack of prioritization.

Death by a thousand cuts

From conception, good ideas in many firms run the gauntlet. They get shaped, molded and trimmed over time, to become more acceptable and less risky. Often, an idea that seemed radical at first is almost unrecognizable by the time it manifests, losing a great deal of what made it interesting along the development process. Defining an idea's vision, and remaining true to that vision throughout the development and delivery process, is vital if the idea is to have value at the end of the process.

Conclusion

Regardless of your innovation approach, methods, tools or frameworks, these fault lines exist in any business and must be addressed. If they aren't, the fault lines turn into black holes for your ideas, and will chip away the attributes that made the ideas compelling in the first place. Understanding and addressing each fault line creates a smoother path for innovation delivery.

Jeffrey Phillips is lead consultant for OVO Innovation. www.ovoinnovation.com, innovateonpurpose. blogspot.com

Innovation Challenges in the 21st Century

Susana Pinilla

As a pioneer in Peruvian microfinance, I've established a close relationship with thousands of entrepreneurs who started their businesses by capturing people's needs, and created services or products that satisfy those demands.

Presently innovation, as in the history of humanity, starts by resolving human needs by generating an added value. This concept has been driving evolution since time began, guaranteeing subsistence and progress. In the 21st Century, global human interactions open new horizons for innovation with new ways of offering better or faster services, elaborating cheaper or more comfortable products, creating new ones or perfecting the ones that already exist, and adapting them to different cultures.

The delivery of innovation has various phases:

Creating a solution that fills a need
This is the invention or innovation in itself. It begins with a theoretical proposal, often designed on paper although a microbusiness can launch itself directly into the market and use a trial-and-error method.

Prototyping the product/service experience
This is when the difficulties start for small or individual inventors due to a general lack of financial resources. Micro and Small Enterprises (MSEs) start with small loans from family or friends; the financial system doesn't typically finance new economic activities. Hence thousands of inventions remain on paper.

Patenting the invention/innovation
The authorship of the invention and any benefits that this would bring in the future is guaranteed by patenting it in the appropriate institution for registering intellectual property. The high costs and the complex procedures often frustrate young innovators. Consequently, most MSEs don't patent their inventions, which get copied by others who then benefit from their work.

Producing the invention (with two options)
- The inventor sells the invention to a company that produces a similar type of product or service. Most companies prefer to own the invention and will buy the patent (if the inventor has one), can facilitate price negotiation for the invention, but the inventor stays anonymous and loses the intellectual property.

- The inventor develops the project on his or her own. Some bolder innovators become entrepreneurs and self-implement the production of the service or product. It's harder, but also more gratifying. However, creative genius doesn't equate with businesslike discipline and perseverance. It also requires financing for qualified staff, technology, permanent design and marketing.

Promoting the invention to guarantee a short- and medium-term market
Keep in touch with enterprises and consumer groups, get the product or service out and about and assure demand.

Selling the invention
If there's demand, sales progress until the product becomes popular with consumers, and has constant production and monthly sales.

Innovation is hard work for universities, private enterprise and the government alike. From contest funds to finance the prototype, to getting patents and implementing updated technology, to joint venture with serious field enterprises who recognize intellectual property and are willing to share the management and the earnings with the inventor. Likewise, guarantee funds are needed to introduce the idea of innovation credits to the financial system.

The SMEs and young people in Peru and elsewhere are incredibly creative and innovative, which is why we must set an example by being innovative in the products and services we give them.

Susana Pinilla is an anthropologist, business manager, a specialist in employment, inclusive development and competitiveness, and a pioneer in microfinance in Peru.

Opening Windows

Lex de Rooi

Innovation has become a buzzword. Every manager in every company knows that nowadays, the chances of survival are limited if there's no innovation. So we innovate—at least, that's what we think. Genuinely innovative businesses are recognized by a few clear criteria: openness, collaboration, drive, transparency and consistent stimulation from the top. I'd like to focus on just one of those aspects—collaboration.

Collaboration can be optimized; there are various software packages on the market for this very purpose. But installing the software and then thinking that everything will work out is a common delusion. It's not just facilitating a process; there has to be a complete culture turnaround that can never be too far reaching. There will always be plenty of difficult obstacles to surmount.

Every company today tries to innovate with the client in focus, but open windows are needed for this. I know from experience this isn't always easy. Many listed companies have executives and IT departments who share a wary, dismissive view of employees actively participating in social media on a daily basis. Yet, this shows that they don't comprehend how social media brings familiarity with consumer opinions and attitudes.

Social Collaborative Platforms are promising; such systems expedite the basics of teamwork, and allow collusion on innovative projects. But the platforms also embed teamwork in a social context where people can chat, exchange recipes and ideas, and most importantly pass on what's being said about you in the big bad world outside so you can quickly react and respond.

I am convinced that social media will exponentially increase the power of the consumer. For instance, the ethical concepts are increasingly more important to the English consumer when buying food than being organic. This development has an immediate impact on company organization. It isn't a threat—quite the opposite. It opens up opportunities for co-creation projects with consumers that often result in real innovative products. Innovation Jams and Social Brainstorming will soon be commonplace.

What's lacking at the moment is knowledge—particularly amongst senior management. The thought line often still runs along conventional processes and marketing techniques. Which is understandable, but the social media landscape is far more complicated than that. Recent American research lists the advantages of opening windows as follows:

- Senior leaders become leaders who care

- Managers provide feedback and dialogue

- Communication becomes frequent and authentic

- A voice that matters is recognized and heard

- Learning and growth opportunities emerge

- A greater focus on customer satisfaction develops

- Cross-business collaboration improves

- Real quality relationships are realized

Innovating is done from the outside in—a lesson Philips learnt years ago. Now, it's the plucky manager's turn to open the windows wide and conquer the world they find out there.

Lex de Rooi is Chairman of POPAI—Marketing at Retail & Benelux platform voor Shoppermarketing and former VP of Marketing and Communication at Philips.

It's Not a Failure—It's a Learning Experience!

Nick Sawbridge

It is often stated that nine out of ten new products fail; others have claimed that it takes 3,000 ideas to achieve one commercial success. There are so many definitions of *new*, *success* and *failure* that any of these findings could be challenged...yet no one disputes the general belief that there are more failures than successes, and that achieving real breakthroughs is difficult—very difficult.

Although it sounds like a mother saying, "Don't give up, dear!" as her child learns to ride a bike, each failure really does bring success closer. Empirical scientists don't expect every experiment to succeed, so they analyze the reasons for failure and try to correct them. Business, however, views failure like death; it threatens careers. Managers who sense failure hurry to disassociate themselves from projects, and immediately start something new to sound positive and confident about. There's a lot of truth in the old saying that success has many parents, but failure is an orphan.

I've seen test markets fail because a product manufactured in a pilot plant didn't perform properly; despite an easy fix, the entire test was junked. I've seen concepts bomb in research when changing just two words would have overcome the issue. I've seen strong purchase and repeat purchase scores discarded because they didn't come in fast enough.

The management teams all knew why these problems occurred, Yet it wasn't so much fear of the financial effects of failure, but of plummeting personal reputation, that resulted in no one doing the obvious: identifying the problem, figuring out how to correct it, and re-launching.

No one wants to fail. It's expensive and time consuming, just as developing and researching the idea was, so view a market launch problem as a step in the process and not the last stage. Analyze what needs to change, change it and try again.

Failure gives you real world market experience and that brings the old nine out of ten fail metric down to much more manageable odds—the sort of odds that careers and empires grow from, not hide from!

__Nick Sawbridge__ has worked in brand management and advertising as well as innovation consultancy for the last 20 years. He now lives and works in the United States. www.rapidiceusa.com

Rapid Methods for Competitor and Customer Research

Aruna Shekar

New market feasibility methods that are offered to entrepreneurs effectively reduce risk, which increases both success and the speed of market and product evaluation at the front-end of product innovation. We educate tertiary students and assist startup companies to apply suitable techniques and methods for initial market assessments that are often missed out yet are critical to any new product venture.

Product development is a decision-making process; good information is required to make sound decisions with important implications. Startups and small to medium enterprises (SMEs) face enormous financial risks during new product development. A key element of risk minimization is an early emphasis on quickly gathering information about competition.

The prospect of expected research costs, lack of expertise, limited in-house resources and financial pressures to rush to market can often overwhelm SMEs. Too often a more conventional path is chosen, whereby a solution is developed and tested in the market to "see if it works". Such less effective methodologies subject the companies to even greater financial risks.

Web resources such as YouTube and chat forums help companies rapidly research customers and competitor products in a cost-effective manner. A quick online patent search also provides similar useful information on products already in the market. YouTube videos often give detailed information on features and designs about competitors' products, and can be used by entrepreneurs to advertise their own innovations to a wide audience of potential buyers.

YouTube produces a number of relevant topics that are highly beneficial to the ideation process. Expected results for a typical product search include competitor products, homespun innovations and a variety of related needs and problems that can lead to ideas for new products. The video clips provide both powerful visual images and audio commentary that can be archived for later review. Additionally, there are detailed mechanisms and animations available. These provide quick information on competitor offerings, so the designer can focus on features that are unique without "re-inventing the wheel".

The limitations of this method are mainly related to how many results the search engine can obtain. A simple run chart to track the relevance of search results can provide an easy guide to suggest when the efficacy of the review process has diminished.

The videos were reviewed and quickly determined to be "relevant" to the search topic, or "not relevant". Relevance was determined based on the definition of videos containing bicycle carriers (example project, J.McIntyre 2010). A simple ratio of relevant vs. non-relevant topics was plotted such that the efficacy of the exercise could be monitored.

Modern Internet resources like YouTube and chat forums speedily provide information required at the early stages of product development. These virtual methods are more suited to niche products that have their users scattered across the globe (such as extreme sports), and users who tend to communicate online, are generally quite tech-savvy and willing to share their experiences and ideas. Also, these resources provide information that addresses many perceived barriers to early market research. Initial concepts can be compared and contrasted against existing competitors in a rapid and affordable manner. In addition to benchmarking data, online resources can be a valuable source for observing user innovations, and getting feedback for existing products. A focused effort within established limits is recommended for optimal results.

Aruna Shekar is Senior Lecturer in Product Development at Massey University's School of Engineering and Advanced Technology, New Zealand. seat.massey.ac.nz/personal/a.shekar/

Stop Asking for Ideas!

Stephen Shapiro

What if one simple change could have a massive impact on your organization's ability to innovate? If you want to be more innovative, stop asking for ideas and instead focus your energies on a more important skill—asking better questions. Albert Einstein reputedly said, "If I had an hour to save the world, I would spend 59 minutes defining the problem and one minute finding solutions." From my perspective, most organizations spend 60 minutes of their time finding solutions to problems that just don't matter. Too much energy is invested in things that are not real value-creators. That's why many innovation efforts fail. If you take the time to define the "real" problems, challenges, and opportunities for your organization, you'll massively accelerate your innovation efforts.

There are various challenges, ranging from technical challenges on creating a particular chemical compound, to marketing challenges on describing your product for an optimal increase in market share, to HR challenges around improving employee engagement. These challenges can be found anywhere—from customers, employees, shareholders, consultants, vendors, competitors, the list goes on. Organizations have no shortage of challenges.

Unfortunately, some of the most important challenges to solve are hidden due to organizational blind spots and assumption making. So, the "meta-challenge" for organizations is to find out which challenges, if solved and implemented, create the greatest value. Given that organizations have limited resources and money, prioritization is critical.

The first steps in making innovation a reality involve surfacing, identifying, and codifying challenges, and then valuing, prioritizing, and framing those challenges. Think of your innovation portfolio as you would a financial investment portfolio. You want some safe bets (incremental innovation) and some riskier investments (radical innovation). You also want a variety of innovations ranging from technical challenges, marketing challenges, and service challenges to performance improvement challenges.

Of course, value is only created when you find and implement solutions. Framing the challenge is only the first step. But as Einstein noted, if time is taken to define your challenges properly, then workable solutions will be found much more easily.

Innovation isn't about one-time change, but on-going and sustainable change. An organization's ability to change hinges on continually identifying its most pressing challenges. My mantra is, "When the pace of change outside your organization is faster than the pace within, you'll be out of business." And as we all know, today's pace of change is crazier than ever. When done right, a culture of innovation can give you a leg up in a highly evolving marketplace.

Stephen Shapiro *is the author of* Personality Poker: The Playing Card Tool for Driving High Performance Teamwork and Innovation *and* Best Practices Are Stupid: 40 Ways to Out-Innovate the Competition. *www.SteveShapiro.com.*

Empower Every Member of Society to Innovate

Robert-Jan Smits

Imagine a new Europe where ideas and businesses flourish, people live longer, healthier and happier lives and are empowered to breathe new life into ideas and turn challenges into opportunities. Imagine Europe as an Innovation Union...

You might say it is impossible. But, to quote Theodor Herzl: "If you will, it is no fairytale". We can join forces and make it happen. In October 2010, the European Commission presented the blueprint for an Innovation Union. Today, both the European Parliament and the European Council have endorsed it and actions are underway to make it happen.

The Innovation Union consists of concrete commitments to strengthen the knowledge base, get good ideas to market, maximize social and territorial cohesion, collaborating to achieve breakthroughs and to leverage our policies externally. For instance, we aim to create an innovation-friendly environment fit for the 21st Century through setting faster standards and providing more affordable patents, more public procurement of innovative products and services, better access to capital and a true European knowledge market.

We've taken full account of the changing nature of innovation and are active in design thinking, user-driven innovation, public sector innovation and social innovation. We began implementing a new way of pooling resources, bringing together initiatives at the European, national and regional levels for business, civil society and academia under an overarching objective, such as adding two healthy life years to Europe's citizens.

The Innovation Union will empower each and every member of society to become an innovator and drive change. Join us in making the Innovation Union happen!

Robert-Jan Smits *is Director-General of DG Research & Innovation, European Commission.*

Do-It-Yourself:
Don't Get It Wrong!

Klaus-Peter Speidel

"Give a man a fish and you will feed him for a day. Teach a man to fish and you will feed him for a lifetime."

As this saying illustrates, the question of DIY (Do-It-Yourself) is essential for Innovation Delivery. Anyone trying to bring an innovation to market should think about what they want to allow their customers to do themselves, and what they want to do for or with them.

Many major innovations of the 20th century have involved systematic DIY. I suspect that every business has a place for DIY. But no business is DIY all the way through. Even McDonald's doesn't make you cook the burgers. Like selling hamburgers, most businesses involve many steps. At each step you can either let customers do it themselves or do it for them.

DIY is powerful for at least four reasons:

- It addresses the fundamental drive for autonomy and choice (television vs. cinema, the automobile vs. the train, booking travel online vs. the travel agency)

- It decreases costs (fast food, self-service at gas stations, online shops, online check-in)

- It speeds things up

- It's more scalable

But each of the promised benefits involves a risk:

- There are cases where customers are so overwhelmed by choice that they end up buying less. Barry Schwartz, who authored *The Paradox of Choice,* thinks that this is why real-estate agents thrive. Buying a house is so complex that you need someone to walk you through your options (no pun intended).

- If your service or product is perceived as complex, be careful. In many cases, large business-customers will willingly accept higher cost for more service. If customers repeatedly ask you: "Will you help me do this or that?" your answer should eventually be "Yes, of course!", even if it means an extra charge.

- DIY can slow things down (like customers who pack their own shopping bags). In some places and at some times, speed doesn't matter. In a busy supermarket at lunchtime—it matters.

- If any of the above is a major problem, you won't need to scale.

The first startup I was involved in, hypios, organizes problem-solving competitions for R& D issues and invites contributions from appropriate experts. DIY was an important element in hypios' go-to-market strategy; the company has a partially automatic process to identify experts online, which makes a DIY approach possible. We essentially wanted to offer our customers lower service costs.

How did we implement DIY? We went for online sales. Once hypios had established their trustworthiness, solution seekers got an ID and password, could post problems and (anonymously) interact with experts on the hypios platform until a solution could be found.

Our idea was to be the eBay of problem solving, connecting and protecting. We helped find problem solvers, providing the infrastructure and legal framework that ensured no solutions were used without payment. This was considered highly disruptive in the Open Innovation market; all our large competitors had mandatory consulting teams.

What happened?

- Corporate customers can't take the same liberties that non-business customers can. Among other things, they can't use corporate money like we use personal cash or credit. They need to go through extensive levels of validation; so pure online sales don't work.

- Getting help in solving problems from outside the company wasn't as simple as it looked. Companies needed legal and cultural assistance to implement the process. My article "Problem Description in Open Problem Solving" in *The Guide to Open Innovation and Crowdsourcing* sums up how to overcome cultural and cognitive roadblocks in the process. If we wanted to close any sales at all, we needed to explain hypios very precisely to experts inside and outside the company.

- Customers needed assistance in both forming and solving problems. Selling a product on eBay may be easy, but formulating a problem or a solution for an R&D issue isn't.

- Fortunately large business customers weren't as price-sensitive as private consumers.

We introduced a subscription model that included consulting services. We now insist on key differentiation points other than price, such as our technology and the nature of the consulting services we offer. For now, hypios' experience with this new model has been positive. The lessons we've learned:

- Evaluate your market not only in terms of needs, but also find the most appropriate way to serve those needs.

- Figure out what your customers are ready to do themselves, and what they need you for.

- Don't confuse willingness to do something (maybe in exchange for lower prices) with readiness. In our case, there were customers that wanted to use our service as it was, but weren't ready to do so.

- Look at how earlier players did it; find out if there were deep reasons for doing it their way and if those reasons still hold. In the case of open problem solving for corporate customers, there was a deep reason to offer consulting services. Customers were not ready. Using our service implied a large number of cultural and cognitive changes. To make sure the first experience was a success, we needed to help them implement the test. We were wrong when we thought that earlier competitors just wanted to generate more cash. In airplane travel, for example, Ryanair and Easyjet were among the first to identify a host of services that customers no longer needed and were willing to give up for lower prices.

Klaus-Peter Speidel is Co-Founder of hypios.

Reduce Randomness with Leadership, Creativity and Insight

Wim van Steenkiste, Veronique Bockstal

Randomness will always have a key role in delivering innovation. Mixing leadership, creativity and insight into processes during the different stages of innovation delivery can reduce it. We identify six phases of innovation delivery: our last, but not least important factor is creating ideal environments where these processes can succeed.

Nowadays, only a few ideas turn into a market success. This could lead to the conclusion that luck plays a crucial part in delivering innovation, especially since there is no single solution or formula for finding ways to improve the success rate of delivering innovation. Trying to find a magic formula is always tempting, particularly when randomness comes into play. Nobel Prize winners Fisher Black and Myron Scholes invented a mathematical equation for pricing options and tried to find one unique formula to grasp market randomness in financial markets. It didn't work. The formula's application nearly led to a meltdown of the financial markets. So we don't aim for a single solution, but many co-existing solutions. Whichever one works best for you depends on the DNA of your organization or the individuals involved.

In our experience, successful innovation delivery demands an interaction of three key processes: leadership, creativity and insight.

Leadership
From the many good definitions, we prefer one used by PepsiCo—leadership means driving a change process by "defining a vision", "setting the agenda" and "taking others with you".

Creativity
Creativity helps distance oneself from the "frustration and challenge" of a given problem and postpones logical judgment via an environment where free expression and thinking is allowed and stimulated. Bouncing non-contextual thoughts off other people, creating new alleys and pathways of ideas, and stimulating new associations are at the core.

Insight
Insight is a combination of understanding the hard facts and data with the curiosity and drive to find out more. It demands high energy and a great deal of time; achieving a 360-degree understanding of the problem or situation can lead to almost obsessive behavior.

We identify six different phases of innovation delivery:

- Frustration. During this phase, the insight process dominates the overall innovation process.

- Hunch. Relative techniques and processes are now getting involved, helping to shape new ideas that respond to the previous frustration.

- Concept. The hunch gets translated into a concept. We call this "making the intangible tangible", borrowing the expression from Theodore Levitt.

- Concept with a home. Smart innovation leaders can hijack time and budgets from other projects that were approved by the overall company strategy and organizational system. They reposition the solution so it has a chance of being accepted. CFOs tend to demand upfront, definite proof of real market success, killing the potential of the idea by not letting it find a home where it can develop further. Good leaders know how to influence the corporate agenda to more readily gain access to seeding capital.

- Beta-solutions. Translation of the concept with a home into a beta-solution, its most dangerous stage of existence. The idea is out in the open now, unproven yet extremely vulnerable. The realities of adaptation to market demand high creative skills and good insight processes to monitor and evolve the beta-version.

- Market entry. Cost-cutting during the beta-solution and rollout phases is the worst thing to do. Scale economies aren't initially present; in an attempt to match the correct market price versus initial production costs, "tweaking" occurs, undermining the initial concept.

It's important to embed these processes in the right organizational culture. We need a stimulating environment where randomness can prosper more readily. For example, a company or organization's physical location could have a more significant effect than generally assumed. The right context should allow for slack in management time; successful companies like Google are renowned for giving their associates 20% slack time. The third important environmental factor that contributes to a fertile ground for delivering innovation has to do with corporate culture—cultivating a winning culture means cultivating space for failure.

Wim van Steenkiste and Veronique Bockstal are Partners at Experts@Business. www.expertsatbusiness.be

Elements of Innovation Delivery Effectiveness

Marc de Swaan Arons

One oft-told adage in marketing circles, reported to have come from an ex-CEO of Gillette, goes, "We know that France and Argentina are different—we just treat them the same way!" No matter who said it, it's a truism that many marketers can relate to as the number and importance of global brands continues to explode and CMOs must create successful global marketing organizations.

One key component of success is the relationship between marketing teams charged with developing an innovation at local and global levels. A global mindset is imperative. One executive who is now the CMO of one of the world's biggest CPG companies, smiled broadly as he told how a decade ago he could kill off any pan-European proposal just by telling his Austrian marketing director that the proposed route was the same one the Germans intended to take.

Companies can build marketing organizations with the proper structure, mindset and operating behaviors to achieve a successful balance between local and global initiatives. Diageo and GSK are good examples of this, and more companies can do it. Below are some of the most important elements of global innovation effectiveness:

Connect
All marketers must share a common understanding of the market reality and destination at local and global levels. Connecting requires building trust and an interdependent mindset. Key local teams need to know and believe that their market's success drives the global team's work. Global teams need to be confident that looking for similarities, not differences, is how the local marketers work.

Peter Kirkby, a VP of global marketing, says, "Innovation improved significantly with this approach. Overall business rose from 3% to 14%." Members of newly created future teams, comprised of globally focused marketers steeped in brand and market expertise as well as general country managers working in the top five markets of each global brand, were charged with building sales of designated global brands through innovation and wise use of resources.

Focus
Vigilant focus on, and commitment to, an agreed-upon set of priorities is crucial. Understanding that, the new Coors Light global leadership team recently started to coordinate its big marketing initiatives, and developed a one-page document outlining the brand vision, mission and strategy. Introducing a dashboard with hard metrics, making global marketing and innovation as accountable as any other part of the business, works well to get everyone facing the same direction.

Organize
One common pitfall is not clarifying roles and responsibilities early on. Defining the operating model and roles of each marketing team is important; enforcing the model and required behaviors is even more so. I can't count the number of major initiatives where it was agreed post-evaluation that it would have been better to have taken a step back and clear things up.

Build
Growth and efficiencies accelerate when a company's marketers are on the same page and build on each other's successes and mistakes. Cultivate that behavior by creating a community of excellence—a resource for members to share, find support and counsel each other. To reinforce this, leaders need to reward specific behaviors and develop processes and attitudes that encourage communication. In 2007, marketers working on the OMO soap brand created a so-called "Dirty Club", a global community that supports everyone working on OMO around the world. Podcasts, videos and e-mail bulletins were used to communicate strategy and demonstrate implementation. The brand's intranet site is also a one-stop online resource for all brand vision and strategy documents, links to all their advertising and examples of various successful activation programs around the world.

Basic resources like tools and templates for brand planning and market implementation, as well as a phone and e-mail address directory for all team members, are also housed there.

Simple in concept but complex in execution, these drivers of global marketing effectiveness provide an important framework on which global brand executives can build an organization whose employees work with a proper mindset, act with the appropriate behaviors and possess the required tools for success—at every level. Think of a Starbucks cappuccino: it's the same around the world but local baristas, whether in Singapore or Stuttgart, make it an intensely personal purchase. These ideas underpin Dove's successful "Campaign for Real Beauty", which challenged traditional beauty stereotypes in more than 30 countries by showing "real" women in their underwear. Global brands are the wave of the present and future: No longer will an Austrian marketing director dare to kill an initiative simply because his German colleague planned to take the same route.

Marc de Swaan Arons is Chairman of Marketing Consultancy, EffectiveBrands. This article is an extract from an earlier article entitled "Five Key Drivers of Global Marketing Effectiveness."

Business Case for Successful Innovation Delivery

Laurence Tanty

"The Company" is a leading manufacturer of plastic crates, and has a proven product design track record. But when faced with the challenge of convincing a retailer to invest significant capital for the first time in a fleet of plastic crates for produce logistics, winning the contract came down to how well we made the business concept go live.

The solution significantly changed the way fresh produce transits from supplier to store. The traditional one-way cardboard boxes were replaced by a fleet of custom designed, reusable plastic crates, operating in a closed loop between suppliers, retail distribution centers and stores. This involved designing and manufacturing a range of new crates, implementing software to track the crates, setting up wash centers and securing a financial lease.

The success was confirmed by great customer satisfaction and the contract's rapid extension to a value of over 50 million pounds. What made this particular innovation delivery successful?

Pitching to the right level of decision maker
In this case the head of the business wanted to finance the new fleet without capital investment. We therefore worked with a bank to respond to this hurdle. Pitching to the decision maker or someone who's threatened by change wouldn't have identified this challenge, and have lowered our chances of success.

The retailer's needs were central to our solution: It took twelve months and enormous effort to understand the constraints of the situation and validate a tailored solution. We built a solid business case with facts modeled to the retailer's specifics and provided reassurance by visiting existing service centers as well as the Design Centre.

Listening to users

We built relationships with the supply chain director, the warehouse staff and store staff because their buy-in to the design and handling of the crates, as well as the process flow, would ultimately be key to endorsement.

Having a senior champion in "The Company" is important: As Managing Director of "The Company", I personally championed the initiative and secured buy-in of shareholders. If there's no support from the head of a business to innovation leads, failure will result. Beware of this in organizations with a limited innovation track record—nice words from the top are not enough!

Our initiative was kept under a separate business unit with a dedicated team. The financial performance was measured throughout the process to the specific performance criteria of this market and business unit. If it's included within the company's core business, there's a risk of applying performance criteria that's not relevant to a startup, and it'll lose the focus as well as real success. Consider running a separate business for those true innovations you really care about!

Laurence Tanty worked for Mars Inc., Sara Lee Corp. and more recently at Linpac Group, and applied innovation best practice to B2B logistic packaging.

Top Three Mistakes in Open Innovation Delivery

John Tao

There are three main mistakes made by companies in their open innovation programs.

Lack of alignment

The number one mistake is a failure to align with their organization's business strategy. Everything open innovation involves—partnering with other companies and organizations, protecting intellectual property, licensing, and early business development—must be responsive to the business strategy, otherwise problems arise.

For instance, someone in research may have a good idea, reads that Professor X is working in the field, and initiates a relationship. The work goes well until a year or so later when the business group finds out and says, "Whoa! This isn't consistent with our business strategy." This can happen with pure technology-push projects.

Bottom-up approach

Mistake number two is thinking the innovation effort can be done from the bottom up, that any researcher can initiate an external project by him or herself. It's first a budget issue, then one of alignment. There has to be an agreement on the percentage of the total R&D budget to be set aside for costs associated with the innovation effort. At a minimum, you need the CTO and ideally the CEO to agree it's the right thing to do. Otherwise, the open innovation leader will end up having to beg the people with money to give him some—which means they'll have to cut somewhere.

Over-enthusiasm

The third mistake is being so eager to do a deal that you'll do a bad deal. Sometimes inexperienced negotiators won't want to admit there's no deal, and the one they force to fit later blows up. Instead, you need to do your homework so you know the deal's true, total value. A deal has to bring enough value to satisfy both parties. Negotiators also need to understand what I call the BATNA—the Best Alternative To No Alternative—their alternative to walking away. But they still have to be able to walk away, and not let greed get the better of them.

You need to be patient. Open innovation is a journey—you can't change a company's culture from a closed to open innovation system overnight. It takes time.

John Tao has managed open innovation for 25 years, first at Air Products, then at Weyerhauser and, more recently, in his own open-innovation consultancy, O-Innovation Advisors LLC. www.o-innovation.com

Experimenting, Reinventing the Wheel and Talking with Friends

Suzanne Verdonschot

A youngster who works as a cashier in a supermarket notices that customers sometimes take cases of beer or packages of diapers without paying for them. This affects the weekly turnover. She discusses this issue with a friend who works for another supermarket belonging to a different chain. It becomes clear that the other supermarket has developed a specific system to prevent customers from taking products without paying. This system requires the cashier to type in a number that's visible at the bottom of the cart into their cash system, before they can scan the next customer's products. The only way to see the number is to check the bottom of the cart. By doing so, they're forced to automatically check whether products that haven't yet been scanned are still lying in the cart. She thinks the approach used in her friend's store is very smart. She adopts this way of working to her own supermarket—not by implementing the technical system, but by teaching her colleagues to habitually check the bottom of the cart. The new approach contributes to reduce the turnover loss.

The above story is a real example of an innovation initiative at a supermarket. In the last few years I've traced innovation initiatives like this in various contexts, both in work environments that predominantly consist of higher educated employees (who are traditionally seen as knowledge workers) and work environments where employees aren't typically seen as knowledge workers like the supermarket (where many youngsters work) or home care (where many older women work), where employees are extremely skilled but often don't have a formal education.

A couple of elements from the supermarket example intrigue me:

- A young employee who encounters a problem at work starts this innovation initiative. She identified it as a problem because she had insight in the weekly turnover rates (that the manager writes down on a sheet in the canteen).

- The innovation initiative isn't a completely new idea. She actually took an existing solution and adapted it for the situation at hand.

- The cashier didn't use any formal system of knowledge sharing. She talked about it with a friend and learned from her approach.

- She didn't encounter any problems in experimenting with this new system, nor did she ask permission. She just tried it out and observed the results.

I derived the following lessons for the realizing innovation from this example:

- The importance of tracing difficult or intriguing problems at the work floor. Employees closest to the work know exactly what sort of problems they encounter. These can form a starting point for innovation, and contribute to its successful delivery.

- A curiosity for different approaches, invented in other teams in other contexts, and the desire to learn from them.

- The personal employee network is an important source for knowledge sharing.

- The innovation cycle resembles an experimenting cycle that may contain different phases. The first phase consists of a single experiment where a new approach is tested, adapted, and re-tested. The second phase consolidates a successful approach in day-to-day practice. The third phase comprises the adoption by other entities (e.g. other shops). The second and third phase refer to the actual delivery of innovation.

These lessons differ from an earlier conception of innovation that a successful innovation needs to be 'rolled out' and 'implemented'. This may be attractive from the perspective of controlling employee actions and regulating work processes. However, from the perspective of knowledge development, it's more promising to see innovation as a process of ongoing experimentation where employees can take the lead. It might seem inefficient (employees reinvent the wheel all the time) and unpredictable (employees do not rely on a database or formal procedures, but on people they trust). However, this is rather effective from a learning perspective.

Suzanne Verdonschot is a researcher and consultant who studies and enables innovation in the workplace, and works with Kessels & Smit, The Learning Company. www.kessels-smit.com

Delivery is Technical Proof with a Strong Business Case

Asbjørn van der Vlis

Within IBM, there are several divisions delivering innovation to clients via technical and business innovative solutions. One of these divisions, the Center for Advanced Studies, is set up to both improve the exchange of knowledge between universities, businesses and governmental institutions, and enhance the collaboration and application of scientific/business research for an increase in their innovation process. The Amsterdam Center for Advanced Studies offers a portfolio of programs promoting research and business model innovation to deliver concrete innovative solutions to IBM clients.

One of these programs, Extreme Blue, brings together the creativity and talent of students and experts from IBM to work on a real strategic business challenge given by an IBM client. Four interns come from different cultural backgrounds and universities throughout the Netherlands, and undergo a tough selection process at IBM to qualify for participation. A project team consists of three technical interns, one business intern, an IBM project manager, a technical mentor and a business mentor. The mentors are to assist and challenge; the students are responsible for delivering a technical feasible solution, demonstrated by a proof of concept and a business case showing the economic value of the chosen solution. Extreme Blue is a seasonal, 3-month IBM internship program.

In the first week of Extreme Blue, the four students are sent to one of IBM's clients to receive their strategic challenge. The challenge given is usually broad and requires the students to use their creativity to find the most valuable solution. They do this by using the open innovation process of narrowing down 40 possible solutions to ten, three and finally after research and client collaboration one "golden" idea/solution. The business student will start researching the market to create business models and analyses proving that the chosen solution is marketable and profitable. The three technical students will start developing their proof of concept supported by technical evidence to show the feasibility of their solution.

This approach has been used with many clients via close collaboration for the past six years, and we try to accelerate the innovation process by combining strong expertise from the students, IBM and the acting client.

One of Extreme Blue's clients in 2009 was a financial institution who presented the following challenge: "How can we make group finances simple, transparent and easy to use?" Meaning when groups share costs, think of dinner at a restaurant, jointly buying a present for a friend, group activities etc., a user-friendly payment system should be offered. A friendly group payment solution would save time, money and improve the group's financial relationship. After 12 weeks, using both IBM's technical and the client's financial expertise, the students presented a system allowing payers to make direct transactions via mobile phone. If a group was presented with a bill, for example after dinner in a restaurant, one of the group could take a picture with a mobile phone, select the group member's meal from a menu, where after the bill is directly converted to digital data in the phone via OCR, allowing the user to select the items desired and send it to each group member to do likewise. When all the meal items are selected the costs can automatically be deducted from the user's bank account after user approval. This is fast and easy for both the user and the restaurant offering this transaction service.

Not only was there a technical proof of concept but also a strong business case proving highly profitable benefits to the client that offers this service. At the moment this application is being piloted and further developed while certain parts of the solution are already on the market. This is only one example of the Extreme Blue program; a great way to show how ideas can be translated into innovative and feasible solutions.

Asbjørn van der Vlis is *Innovation Program Manager for Global Business Services, IBM.*

Knowledge Workers, Dynamic Managers and Flexible Organizations

Henk Volberda

62% of companies in the Netherlands are currently focusing on efficiency and other short-term performance criteria. For instance, recent research in the Erasmus Competition and Innovation Monitor showed that the development of new products, services and radical innovations in the Netherlands decreased by 5% between 2009 and 2010. Simultaneously, turnover from new products and services decreased by almost 3%. This data indicates that companies, at least in the Netherlands, focus more on the short run. But a closer look gives a more fine-grained picture: ICT-companies and business services firms have a high turnover from new and improved products and services, while construction companies and financial services firms show a low turnover. At the same time, ICT-companies and business services firms score well and construction companies and financial services firms score low on social innovations. Social innovations are new ways of working, managing and organizing that can increase its competitiveness and productivity. While technological innovations explain around 25% of innovation success, social innovations explain around 75%. Organizations with a high score on social innovations perform better on long- and short-term performance criteria, such as innovativeness (+31%), productivity (+21%) and more satisfied employees (+12%).

Social innovations can be categorized into knowledge workers, dynamic managerial capabilities and flexible organizations. The first category is the most important component of social innovations, and aims at fully utilizing employees' talents and competences. Trust within organizations is an important pillar of knowledge workers, encouraging them to increase commitment with their colleagues to come up with good solutions. Dynamic managerial capabilities require accountability (attention of management for targets) on one hand and informal management (autonomy for employees) on the other. For flexible organizations, a high internal rate of change is crucial. Organizations with a high internal rate of change adjust well to processes, products and services in order to react to or anticipate changes in all aspects of the environment.

Investment in knowledge workers, dynamic managerial capabilities or flexible organizations is currently insufficient. Strong investments in these innovations results in high performance. Furthermore, collaboration with other organizations and knowledge institutions is required to further reinforce performance. For example, by collaborating with a knowledge institute, an organization can acquire certain knowledge faster than if it tried to develop that knowledge in-house, and thus collaboration reduces the time-to-market. The Erasmus Competition and Innovation Monitor showed that a high score on social innovations, external collaboration and a considerable amount of internal R&D investments are key to success. By doing this organizations are not only innovative, but also efficient and perform well.

Henk Volberda is Professor of Strategic Management and Business Policy at the Rotterdam School of Mangement, Erasmus University and Director of the top institute INSCOPE: Research for Innovation.

From Invention to Innovation

Albert van der Wal, Hank Reinhoudt

In 2004, we investigated and developed a new desalination technology based on capacitive deionization (CapDI) at Unilever R&D. CapDI is a platform technology ideally suited to remove salt and hardness from brackish and tap water. We originally developed the technology as part of a project to remove hardness from water prior to entering a washing machine in order to improve fabric cleaning. Once we saw the technology's potential, however, we realized that this could potentially be used for a wide range of applications and decided to spin-off a new company, Voltea b.v. The objective of Voltea is to develop and commercialize CapDI technology. In 2006, we convinced Unilever Ventures to make an initial seed investment in our company.

Funding of a startup company

To transform an invention into an innovation requires external capital. Investing in a startup company that owns a breakthrough invention but has neither customer base nor sales is high risk. The key challenge was to convince investors how the invention could lead to commercially successful innovations. The only available source of funding at this early stage of the company was via venture capital. Venture capitalists aim for high returns on investments to compensate for the high risks of early stage companies. They therefore base the decision on investing in an early stage company on the following criteria:

- Unique technology
- Large market potential
- Scalable business model
- A strong management team

One of the key challenges during the investment round was to convince venture capitalists of the huge opportunities in store while the technology was still in the high-risk invention phase. We did this by further developing the invention in parallel with potential customer bases, and demonstrating in feasibility studies that the technology has unique benefits that could lead to successful innovations. By developing a strong patent portfolio, key features of the technology could be protected. This assured investors that potential competitors could be kept out of the market once Voltea was ready to launch a new innovation.

Further investments from Pentair Inc. in 2009 and Rabo Ventures in 2010 followed up the initial investment from Unilever Ventures.

The current status of Voltea b.v.
Voltea was initially based at the Unilever R&D location in the Netherlands. here we could setup the company and write a business plan whereby we still had access to Unilever services for IP support, submission of grant proposals and know-how on manufacturing. Voltea has now developed two lead innovations whereby CapDI will be launched in a cooling tower application to save water, and in whole households as part of a water-softening device. In 2009 the company moved to a science park in Leiden, and since early 2011 has its own building in Sassenheim, currently employing 30 people.

Albert van der Wal and Hank Reinhoudt work for Voltea b.v., a new desalination technology.

Balancing Process and Passion in Innovation Delivery

Katja van der Wal

Innovation is a game of seeking trade-offs. The Innovation Delivery (ID) phase is all about focusing on details in order to get innovation realized. You may face situations that challenge initial assumptions; therefore, managing to deliver the business promise determined in the front-end phase is a real challenge. To be successful in ID is to make the right choices in optimizing and balancing trade-offs.

To make these "right" choices, here at Philips Consumer Lifestyle we focus on the consumer—not just in the early phases or during final product evaluation tests, but throughout the entire innovation process, making small as well as big decisions. For everyone from the various disciplines that take part in the process, it should be clear how their contribution is related to the consumer benefits on all aspects, but especially the high-tech aspects!

Before moving into the ID phase, we aim to establish a realistic commitment of all multi-disciplinary team members. The term "realistic" is key; from the first moment we start with the ID phase, we freeze the specifications that emerged from the front-end phase as well as the project timings and budget. The delivery phase is a real "hard-gated process".

One of the major challenges in upscaling is to retain this commitment and a clear sight of the defined business promise. At Philips CL, Having people who played a central role in the front-end team participating also in the ID team is imperative. Although no longer in the leading role, they can still bring their relevant experience to the table. They can draw on why decisions were made in the front-end and elucidate the consequences of changing the project course when things play out differently than expected. It can sometimes be challenging to motivate these fuzzy front-end champions whilst confining them to a less explorative and more structured ID process. But what matters most in the end for them, is to see "their baby" actually out there in the market.

At Philips CL we follow a "hard-gated process" to structure our innovation activities to mitigate risks and uncertainties inherently associated with innovation. When it comes to the ID phase we have well-established methods, guidelines, and milestones in place to guide innovation teams on their journey. Go-to-market teams work in parallel; since many dependencies arise between the various ID activities, you need a streamlined, established process.

However, one must make sure that embedding methods, guidelines, and checklists in work processes doesn't become "the default" option. It is important to keep questioning what the most effective method is to mitigate associated risks. Processes are a means, not an end. We found that in the ID phase of the SENSEO, regardless of the extensive amount of marketing and consumer research, its market success topped even our most optimistic forecasts. This told us that in ID you can't mitigate every risk. Innovation is and remains uncertain, no matter how well investigated and managed it may be. You only know what it will bring when you've delivered it.

Looking at the future, we're increasingly more aware of the need to think and act more entrepreneurially. We want people to take on their roles and responsibilities as individuals, but even more so collectively, thereby taking ownership of the situation when needed based on their judgment and capabilities. We want people to be passionate about their work and use that passion to make innovation happen. Our crew has so much "drive" for innovation; it's a matter of unleashing that energy towards concrete results. We value people taking their own initiative, using methods and guidelines as they see fit.

Introducing entrepreneurial thinking and acting whilst maintaining structure and discipline to mitigate risks is a tension we must learn to effectively balance in order to get better and faster innovation delivery.

Katja van der Wal is Director for Open Innovation for Philips Consumer Lifestyle.

Innovation Is Not Strategy

Tom Warren

We hear the words Strategy and Innovation thrown around a lot, and often we hear them said together. "We need an innovation strategy," or perhaps "We need a more innovative strategy"—which, of course, is a different animal. The more I've learned about Communities of Practice, the more I've come to understand how innovation happens. And I've come to the conclusion that strategy and innovation aren't made of the same cloth.

Strategy is top-down; Innovation is bottom-up.
In every context I can think of, strategy is about someone at the top of a hierarchy planning what will happen. Innovation is emergent; it happens when practitioners on the ground have worked on something enough to discover a new approach in the messy variety of practitioner effort and conversation. Innovation is, by its nature, unorthodox.

Strategy is defined in advance; Innovation is recognized after the fact.
While a strategy is defined ahead of time, nobody can plan what an innovation will be. In fact, many innovations are serendipitous accidents, or emerge from a side-project that wasn't part of the top-down defined workload to begin with. This is because the string of events that led to the innovation is never truly rational, logical or linear. We often don't recognize the result as an innovation until it's already happened; whether something is an innovation or not depends on its usefulness after it's been experienced in context.

Strategy plans for success in known circumstances; Innovation emerges from failure in unknown circumstances.
Strategy is great for things that have to be carried out with great precision according to known circumstances, or at least predicted circumstances. However, if you dig underneath the veneer of the story behind most innovations, you find that there was trial and error going on behind the scenes, and lots of variety happening before the (often accidental) eureka moment. Even after that moment, the only reason we consider the outcome an innovation is because it found traction and really worked.

Does this mean that all managers can do is cross their fingers and hope innovation happens? No. What it does mean is that having an innovation strategy has nothing to do with planning or strategizing the innovation itself.

Managing for innovation requires a more oblique approach, one that works directly on creating the right conditions for innovation to occur. And that means setting up mechanisms where practitioners can thrive as a community of practice, and where they can try and fail often enough and quickly enough that great stuff emerges. It also means setting up mechanisms that allow the right people to recognize which outcomes have the best chance of being successes—and therefore, end up being truly innovative.

I'm as tired of hearing about Apple as anyone, but when discussing innovation they always come up. We tend to think of Apple as linear, controlled and very top-down. The popular imagination seems to buy into a mythic understanding of Apple, that Steve Jobs had some kind of preternatural design compass embedded in his brain stem. But inside Apple, the strategy for innovation demands that design ideas be generated in multitudes like fish eggs and run through a sort of artificial natural selection mechanism that kills off the weak and only lets the strongest ideas rise to the top.

Google does the same thing. They do a modicum of concept-vetting inside the walls, but they push new ideas out into the marketplace (their "Labs" area) as soon as possible and leverage the collective interest and energy of their user base to determine whether the idea will work or how it should be refined. People don't mind using something at Google that seems to be only half-successful as a design, because they know it'll be tweaked and matured quickly. Part of the payoff of using a Google product is the fun of seeing it improved under your very fingertips.

Tom Warren is a Partner at Kalypso, and focuses on advising global business in the telecommunications, logistics and transportation industries on innovation, strategy, product and operational improvements. www.kalypso.com

Front-End Inspiration for Innovation Delivery Professionals

Gijs van Wulfen

The lack of clarity at the start of the innovation process gave rise to the term "fuzzy front-end" of innovation. Ideas for new products and services could come from anywhere—inside the company through research and development, marketing, sales, the call centre or online sales department, from top management, the relevant line managers or enthusiastic co-workers. But in practice, it's often unclear as to where real innovative ideas should actually come from. What's more, innovation research has found that only one in seven new product ideas are successfully introduced on the market. What happens to the other six? They seem to get stuck in the innovation delivery phase due to a lack of priority or resources, or maybe they just didn't seem feasible.

So the front-end is fuzzy and the back-end isn't very effective. It proves that creating new products, services or even business models is difficult, which is precisely why I like it. Based on my experience at the front-end of innovation, my 3 C's—Connect, Customer, and Creativity—can smooth the innovation implementation process.

Connect
Once an innovation project has passed the initial front-end gates, it becomes one of a multitude. The big question is how to make your project stand out from the crowd and keep the decision makers' attention. I found the answer in the FORTH method. In addition to the core project team, an extended team joined us. The extended team is invited on a personal basis, and represents top decision makers from the business side of the company. The main advantage is that they're fully aware of any progress made; once you are part of a team, you will support the outcome. So connect top decision makers to your project in the innovation delivery phase.

Customers
In innovation, the main struggle often happens within the organization itself. Many colleagues and managers have a full-time job disagreeing on everything. In the FORTH method, we test new product ideas with customers immediately.

In the last step, we concentrate on four new mini-business cases of our most attractive ideas. We use the "voice of the customer" to justify our choices. I suggest you do the same thing during the back-end phase of innovation. Present your concept or prototypes on a regular basis to potential customers, and use their enthusiasm to get a higher priority and more resources internally.

Creativity
Most people associate the front-end phase with creativity and the back end with structured project management—that's history. The front-end phase in the FORTH method is highly structured, and during the back-end phase you need more than PRINCE2 to deliver the innovation project. Although the soul of the innovative concept is created at the front-end, you need to stay flexible and creative throughout the process. More than ever, you need professional brainstorming tools and creativity to deal with complex feasibility issues.

If you are delivering your innovation, make sure you continue using front-end ideation skills during the back-end phase. Do so, and you'll become an even more professional innovator.

Gijs van Wulfen is the author of Creating Innovative Products & Services *and founder of the FORTH innovation method.*

Deliver Creative Solutions Via Digital Labs

Nicole Yershon

At Ogilvy, we aim to introduce our clients and employees to new technology that inspires, enhances and delivers great creative solutions to business and marketing problems. Ogilvy is a communications agency with a global network of digital labs—the Ogilvy Digital Labs—that acts as a hub for partnerships, research, education and knowledge sharing around new media and innovative communications. The Labs can offer clients services such as strategy workshops and trend monitoring, or create a "Lab in a Box" for a client; a bespoke package which may involve building a physical lab space in the client's offices. We offer our clients a calendar of training modules and free events relating to our "semesters of learning".

Our mantra is to create an 80-20% split for innovation, which means clients spend 80% on tried, tested and traditional media while taking 20% to fix a specific problem with the right solution, whatever that may be. An example of this philosophy at work is a recent project called IBM Seer. IBM Seer was the virtual guide to the Wimbledon Tennis Championships 2010, and used augmented reality to supply users with useful information about the event and venue in real-time. It was picked up by the BBC and awarded a Silver Lion at the prestigious Cannes Awards. IBM Seer is the perfect example of how innovative thinking can produce original and effective work.

The Lab is a real room, a physical space with various examples of new technologies: 3D TV screens with and without glasses, 360° screens, tablets, smart phones, Kinect & Xbox gaming, Macs, Emergir kit, digital signage, holograms, augmented reality and much more.

Ogilvy has four physical labs—as well as various virtual labs—and a lab team runs each one. It's a connected network of continuous sharing that ensures help is given in making the impossible possible via our partners in various countries.

The labs also have a their own small R&D pot for funding feasibility checks on new ideas, inspiration, lab days, digital education, ideas that creatives feel passionate about but the client may not necessarily have the budget for, sponsorship of cutting-edge events, conferences, and occasionally the purchase of equipment like iPads, phones, and Kinect.

Some of the labs act as a change agent, holding the client's hand through new media ideas such as augmented reality, so that we can now offer our clients communication not only through TV & print, but also via our partnerships or other Ogilvy disciplines—augmented reality, gaming, mobile, social media and more. The labs are free spaces to conduct experiments and are effective tools for delivering media innovations.

To be innovative you need curiosity, a belief that you are able to make something better, and then a dogged determination to not let anyone stop you until each step has been taken to complete and execute your initial vision. It's all about "making it happen" no matter what.

Nicole Yershon: *"I work hard and am a good person, who treats people with respect." As Director of Innovations at Ogilvy London, "I get it done."*

Innovation Delivery and Road Mapping

Max von Zedtwitz

Imitation and copying is still the prevalent form of innovation in China, not originality and inventiveness. However, imitation per se isn't a bad thing; it's a necessary step in mastering a discipline. Children do it when they go to school and learn grammar and algebra. They aren't expected to develop their own rules and orthography, after all! We expect them to imitate their teachers. Nations do it, and have done it for quite some time. As much as China is seen to be copying the West, just a few decades ago it was the Koreans imitating the Americans and the Japanese, and the Japanese copying the Americans and Europeans. For good measure, in the middle of the 18th Century it was the Americans who copied the British and the French, much to their dismay, without honoring much of their intellectual property (IP) rights. Technological imitation has tradition.

China is moving towards an innovation economy—by its own definition and ambition. For the time being, it is still mostly a manufacturing economy, but pockets of cutting-edge R&D and innovation are emerging. China is already leading any country in the world in total numbers of patents filed, and has assumed leading positions in areas such as material science, physics, and chemistry. In due time, these "pockets"—as small as they appear today—will be the seeds of a scientific and technological revolution.

To many people, the idea of a strong and "innovation-powered" China is somewhat intimidating. An innovative China is a good thing! It is probably just a matter of time until other countries start copying China.

Foreign companies now realize that poor IP enforcement doesn't mean poor R&D. More than 1300 foreign-owned R&D centers were set up in China by the end of 2010. Many of them are in information and communication technology (ICT), but there's also consumer packaged goods, industrials, material science, etc. Most foreign R&D is done in Shanghai and Beijing—the usual suspects, where the main centers of decision-making and China's top universities are. But more R&D is moving inland: GE recently announced it would set up six more R&D centers in central China's Xi'An and Chengdu.

Motorola already has 19 R&D centers all over China. Foreign R&D is now following Chinese intelligence as much as it is following Chinese consumers.

An innovative China will be a wellspring of prosperity not just for China, but also for most of the rest of the world. Pick up your cell phone, open up your laptop, or go for a spin in your car; all these items are the product of technologies that were invented by a multitude of companies in more than a dozen different countries. No single country or company owns the right to these technologies alone. We all benefit from them. Imagine what impact China—or India for that matter—will have on the global stock of science and technology once they too start contributing on an equal basis!

This progress is likely to be carried out mostly by Chinese firms, not just foreign R&D centers in China. The challenge for Chinese firms is to benefit from its own intelligence as much as it benefits from its uniquely advantageous access to its own market. Can they do it? The answer isn't at all trivial. History is plastered with the names of companies that have failed to capitalize on their own innovation power. The hurdles for Chinese companies in the 21st Century may even be higher than those for Western firms in the 20th Century. What can they do? The answer is "road mapping".

Catch up is easy when the road map is clear. At a national level, the Chinese government maps out priority areas and focuses national effort there. Of course overall efficiency may suffer as a result, at the expense of success in particular industries and scientific realms, but having such a clear and consistent national policy is not unique to China or its particular form of government. Other countries have devised similar schemes. In the 1960s and 1970s, it was the MITI's industrial creation policy in Japan. In the 1940 to 1960s, it was the United States with their Manhattan and Apollo programs. China learned from those experiences and developed an approach that, hopefully, will work for China.

At a company level, being an innovation follower is easier than being a leader. Making the switch is a huge strategic challenge. The internal changes are tremendous, implicating new forms of leadership, new incentive systems, new organizational structures, and new ways of doing things. What has served them well to get this far may not be what will let them succeed once they're in front. In ten years we'll know which ones have figured out how to overcome these challenges. They'll be the Toyotas, Microsofts and Googles of the 2020s... and winners in the global race for innovation.

Max von Zedtwitz, *Glorad*

Conclusions

By now you've read a wide variety of views and subjects relating to innovation and entrepreneurship. Though this book may not be an exhaustive compendium of voices and perspectives, I am convinced that it offers important insights on effective innovation delivery and entrepreneurship.

Delivery is key for innovation; that was clear from the outtake of this collection of articles. And there is more to guaranteeing success than just a smart process such as Stage-Gate®, especially since there isn't agreement about what the best approach is. Some experienced managers say that delivery is all about discipline; others say that creativity is of key importance, right through to the end of the delivery phase. A few leading minds proclaim that the most important factor for innovation delivery is the quality of the people, whereas many others feel the entrepreneurial mindset and perseverance are most important. Some make recommendations with a mind to radical or disruptive innovation, while others base their advice on incremental innovation. And although we focus on the so-called back-end of innovation in this book, many contributors agree that there should not be a clear division between the fuzzy front and the rougher realization when it comes to innovation.

In the preceding pages, contributors covered everything from marketing and sales to research & development and finance. They discuss the multidisciplinary face of the innovation team and the importance of collaboration as a focus in its own right. They've only scratched the surface when it comes to disciplines such as metrics, and have perhaps over-considered other areas, such as 'open innovation', as tools for delivering innovations.

One take away from all this is that there is no "one truth," no magic formula for innovation delivery. With so much to consider, you must begin your own "voyage" of exploration and exploitation, and I hope you will use this as a guide for better performance as well as further learning. Because there is so much to say about innovation delivery and entrepreneurship, the conversation should only begin when you close this book.

I encourage everyone to start or continue experimenting (not only in the lab, but out there in the market) and to be open to new developments and different views.

List of Contributing Companies

15inno

2degrees

Aalto

AllianceExperts

Applied Marketing Science Inc.

Australian National University

Beacon Partners

Brabantia

Brand Delivery

Burton Car Company

C2B consultancy

CDTI

Danone

Delft University of Technology

Designlink

Doblin

EffectiveBrands

EIT

Eneco

Enovite

Erasmus

Ericsson

Ernst & Young

EU Advisor

Eureka

European Commission

Expertise Beyond Borders

Experts@Business

FORTH

FrieslandCampina

GE

GlaxoSmithKline

GLORAD

Government of Peru

Holst Centre

hypios

IBM

IMD

IMI

INNOA

Innosight Asia

Innovation Factory

Innovation Leadership Network

innovation-3

Innovationedge

INSEAD

Inspire2Live

jpb.com

Kalypso LLP

Kessels & Smit,
The Learning Company

Kraft Foods

Linpac

London Business School

Mars

Massey University Albany

Merial Limited

MIH Centre

New Product Creation

New York University

North Star Alliance

Nutricia

Ogilvy

OpenTo

Orange Vallée

OVO Innovation

Oxford PharmaScience

p2 project management

paul4innovation

PDMA

Philips

Phronesys

POPAI

Prisma & Partners

pro-Actuate

PRTM

Publishing Research Laboratories

PwC

RapidICE

Rijksuniversiteit Groningen

Royal DSM NV

SafeSpace

Shell

Siemens

Singapore Management University

Taste Tideswell

Temple University

The Agile Enterprise

Triniti Marketing

Twynstra The Bridge

Univé

University of Greenwich

Uppsala University

Vanmoof bicycles

VEDA

Virmax Limited

VODW

Voltea

Waag Society

WD-40

List of Contributing Nations

Australia
Austria
Belgium
Czech Republic
China
Denmark
EU
Finland
France
Germany
India
Italy
Mexico
The Netherlands
New Zealand
Peru
Russia
Singapore
South Africa
Spain
Sweden
Switzerland
UK
USA

Articles by Topic

Collaboration (External), Networking, Open Innovation, Connect and Align,
Co-Development, Networks, Crowd Sourcing
> 5-8, 23, 25-27, 35, 37-39, 46-49, 63, 65-66, 68, 72-73, 78-79,
> 88-89, 97, 99, 134-136, 138, 143, 145, 153-154, 163, 165,
> 169-170-172, 178-179, 190-195, 200-201, 209, 212, 219-222,
> 226-229

C. Knowledge, consumer research, IP
Knowledge, -Collection, -Transfer
> 3-4, 14, 16, 19-20, 40-41, 56, 58, 111-112, 127, 129-131,
> 153-154, 163, 165, 206-207, 223, 225

Needs & Demands, Voice of Customer, Market, Concept, Co-Creation,
Commercialization, Design Thinking
> 7-8, 32, 34, 40-41, 52-53, 56, 58, 78-79, 134-135, 136, 138,
> 143, 145-147, 153-154, 163, 165, 171-172, 176-177, 182-183,
> 192-195, 198-201, 204-205, 208, 213, 215, 219-220, 236-237

Intellectual Property, IP, Patents, Contracts, Licensing
> 74-75, 88-89, 113-114, 141-142, 198-199, 230-231, 240, 242

D. Process
Portfolio, Selections, Funnel
> 27-29, 48, 59-60, 63, 66, 68, 101, 158-159, 201, 206-207,
> 232-235, 247

Process Order and Road Mapping
> 40-41, 52-54-55, 61-62, 102, 105, 143, 145, 148, 150, 160,
> 162, 166, 168, 173, 175-177, 180-183, 198-199, 213, 215,
> 232-233, 240, 242

Discipline, Project Management, Quality Delivery, Efficiency, Scalable
> 44-45, 61-62, 115-116, 130-131, 139-140, 155, 157, 176-177,
> 209, 212, 216, 218, 228-233, 240, 242

Agile, Flexibility, Less Rules/Process
> 40-41, 54-55, 80-81, 97, 99, 120, 122, 143, 145

E. Finance

Index